INFORMATION AND COMMUNICATION TECHNOLOGIES FOR DEVELOPMENT IN AFRICA

Volume 1

Opportunities and Challenges for Community Development

Edited by Ramata Molo Thioune

International Development Research Centre
Ottawa • Dakar • Cairo • Montevideo • Nairobi • New Delhi • Singapore

Council for the Development of Social Science Research in Africa

© International Development Research Centre 2003

Jointly published by the International Development Research Centre (IDRC)
PO Box 8500, Ottawa, ON, Canada K1G 3H9
http://www.idrc.ca

and the Council for the Development of Social Science Research in Africa
(CODESRIA)
PO Box 3304, Dakar, Senegal
http://www.codesria.org
ISBN 2-86978-114-8

National Library of Canada cataloguing in publication data
Main entry under title:
Information and communication technologies for development in Africa.
Volume 1: Opportunities and challenges for community development

Translation of: Technologies de l'information et de la communication pour le
développement en Afrique. Volume 1: Potentialités et défis pour le développement communautaire.

Co-published by CODESRIA.
ISBN 1-55250-001-2

1. Information technology – Africa.
2. Communication in community development – Africa.
3. Community development – Africa.
I. Thioune, Ramata Molo.
II. International Development Research Centre (Canada)
III. Codesria.

HC805.I55I53 2003   338.9'26'096   C2003-980110-1

■ Contents

Chapter 1

Introduction

Chapter 2

The context of ICTs in Africa: The cases of Kenya, Senegal, South Africa, and Uganda

Chapter 3

Information and Communication Technologies: Expectations of African communities

Chapter 4

Use of ICTs: Impacts on African communities

Chapter 5

Introduction and appropriation of ICTs: Challenges and prospects

Appendix 1

Appendix 2

Bibliography

■ Contributors

Agonga, Aquinata, Research Assistant (Kakamega, Kenya*)*.

Etta, Florence Ebam, Senior Program Officer, Acacia, IDRC, Nairobi, Kenya.

Burton, Simon, Senior Lecturer in sociology at the School of Human and Social Sciences at the University of Natal, South Africa.

Katia, Salome, Research Assistant (Makueni, Kenya).

Narathius, Asingwire, Head of Department of Social Work and Social Administration at Makerere University in Kampala, Uganda.

Sène, Khamathe, Consultant Engineer, Dakar, Senegal.

Thioune, Ramata Molo Aw, Knowledge Analyst, Acacia, IDRC, Dakar, Senegal.

Review and comments

Rathgeber, Eva M., Joint Ottawa-Carleton Chair in Women's Studies, University of Ottawa, Canada.

List of figures

List of tables

List of acronyms and abbreviations

Acacia	Communities and Information Society Program of IDRC
AHI	Africa Highlands Initiative
AIDS	Acquired Immunodeficiency Syndrome
ATI	All Taxes Included
CCK	Communications Commission of Kenya
CEEWA	Council for the Economic Empowerment of Women of Africa
CIC	Community Information Centre
CODESRIA	Council for the Development of Social Science Research in Africa
CRC	Community Resource Centre
DSIN	Digital Service Integration Network
ELSA	Evaluation and Learning System for Acacia
ENDA	Environment and Development Action
FASI	Family Support Institute
FLE	Family Life Education
FM	Frequency Modulation
GEEP	Group for Population Study and Teaching
GPF	Women's Promotion Grouping
VCMR	Village Communities Management and Rehabilitation
GSM	Global System for Mobile Communications
IBA	Independent Broadcasting Authority
ICASA	Independent Communication Authority of South Africa
ICRAF	International Agro-Forestry Centre
ICTs	Information and Communication Technologies
IDRC	International Development Research Centre

IP	Internet Protocol
ISP	Internet Service Provider
ITU	International Telecommunications Union
KCL	Kencell Communications Limited
KPTC	Kenya Posts and Telecommunications Corporation
MCT	Multipurpose Community Telecentre
NCS	National Communications Secretariat
NEPAD	New Partnership for Africa's Development
NIC	National Internet Centre
NRM	Natural Resource Management
NGO	Non-Governmental Organization
OSIRIS	Observatoire sur les Systèmes d'Information, les Réseaux et les Inforoutes au Sénégal (Observatory on Information Systems, Networks and Information Highways in Senegal)
PCK	Postal Corporation of Kenya
SAED	Société d'Aménagement et d'Exploitation des Terres du Delta du fleuve Sénégal et des Vallées du Fleuve Sénégal et de la Falémé
SATRA	South Africa Telecommunications Regulation Authority
SCA	Sports and Cultural Association
SENELEC	Société Nationale d'Electricité (National Electricity Company of Senegal)
SENTEL	Sénégalaise de Télécommunications
SME	Small- and Medium-Sized Enterprises
SONATEL	Société Nationale de Télécommunication (National Telecommunications Company of Senegal)
STD	Sexually Transmitted Disease
TKL	Telkom Kenya Limited
TPS	Fondation du Trade Point Sénégal
UNCSTD	United Nations Commission on Science and Technology for Development
UNFPA	United Nations Population Fund
UTL	Uganda Telecom Limited
VAT	Value-Added Tax
VCMR	Village Communities Management and Rehabilitation
WARF	West Africa Rural Foundation

Foreword

Africa is confronted with many challenges. One of the most important of these challenges is to integrate the continent into the information society. Africa's isolation must be overcome by reducing the digital divide and facilitating the continent's absorption into the global information society.

In an avant-garde approach, and convinced that research through the production of learning and applicable knowledge could contribute significantly to a better development, the International Development Research Centre (IDRC) launched a program known as Acacia. This new initiative was exclusively devoted to Africa and was a direct response to appeals from Africans to help pull their continent out of underdevelopment.

By launching the Acacia program, IDRC, enriched with its experience in the area of development research, wanted to contribute to the production of an essentially African body of knowledge on the role of information and communication technologies (ICTs) in the economic and social development process. This body of knowledge and learning was to enlighten decision-making and ease the integration of the continent into the information era.

The Acacia projects that were developed and implemented in partnership with development actors and African researchers were oriented toward learning. This focus on learning and the production and sharing of knowledge is reflected in the systematic documentation and evaluation of Acacia's experiences in sub-Saharan Africa.

This book synthesizes the results of the first "generation" of pilot projects on the introduction of ICTs in poor communities. It highlights the opportunities and challenges that these communities face as they attempt to adopt ICTs as a means of their integration into the new economy. These results are analysed in terms of conditions, processes, methods, and strategies for introducing and appropriating ICTs.

Produced through cooperation between IDRC and African institutions and communities, this volume comes at an opportune time. We hope that its readers will use its findings to turn ICTs into real tools at the service of sustainable development in Africa. By accepting to jointly publish the book, the Council for the Development of Social Science Research in Africa (CODESRIA) also confirms IDRC's partnership approach and its deep conviction that the development of Africa must and can be achieved by and for Africans.

Adebayo Olukoshi
Executive Secretary
CODESRIA

Maureen O'Neil
President
IDRC

Preface

For the past few decades, the international community has noted a growing digital gap between developed countries and Africa, on the one hand, and within African countries, between the elites and the poorer and underprivileged populations, on the other hand.

New information and communication technologies can serve as a development lever to speed up the economic development of Africa and its poor communities. ICTs are also known to transform communities. However, the details of these transformations and the degree and pace of such changes in poor communities have yet to be fully grasped. Equally, the ways in which ICTs might best serve development are still relatively unknown.

Therefore, it is critical to determine the implications that these changes will have for the poor communities that ICTs are supposed to transform. Studies and investigations are needed to generate new hypotheses that can be tested. The results of such research must also be shared rapidly and effectively to keep up with the pace at which ICTs evolve.

In response to Africa's appeal in 1996 at the Midrand Conference in South Africa, in 1997 IDRC initiated the Acacia program to help enlighten African decision-makers and their partners on the fastest and most appropriate ways and means of filling the digital gap between Africa and the rest of the world. Acacia was unique because from the start it was a research program focused on underprivileged or marginalized communities of sub-Saharan Africa. Acacia worked on the hypothesis that ICTs can help poor communities in Africa to find new ways to develop and improve their standard of living. A research-action approach was used to develop projects on themes such as governance, employment and entrepreneurship, natural resource management, and health.

In May 2002 in Nairobi, Kenya, members of the Acacia team met and expressed the urgent need to gather knowledge about the research that had been supported and to disseminate this information on a broad scale. During the same month in Kampala, Uganda, the Evaluation and Learning System for Acacia (ELSA) team met to establish an action plan to assess the research that had been conducted under the Acacia project. These assessments were designed to meet the information needs of both IDRC and its partners. At this meeting, it was decided that to document Acacia's activities, studies focusing on communities should be conducted on a pan-African scale.

Two of the studies (on community telecentres and school networks) dealt with the infrastructure and modalities of gaining access to ICTs. The third study, which is the subject of this book, tried to determine how Acacia and the ICT projects it supported "added value" to the grassroots communities and the development processes they were implementing.

As their contribution to the learning process, the researchers involved in this study try to answer questions on community access to ICTs, access being analysed in the sense of availability, utilization capacity and opportunities for all community members. The study also attempts to respond to interrogations linked to the process of introducing ICTs, to the level of participation of the communities and to their reactions to these new techno-logies. It further proposes some answers to questions relating to the adaptability of ICT technologies and their impacts on the communities.

It is hoped that the findings of this study will help managers in both Acacia and IDRC, as well as their partner organizations, to improve ongoing initiatives and direct future programs. Organizations and researchers working on ICT as well as NGOs, African governments, and donors may also be interested in how these findings can contribute to future ICT programs.

Clearly, the purpose of this study is not to verify Acacia's hypothesis. The research is exploratory and descriptive – with a focus on communities and their reactions to technological innovations that will bring about chan-ges in their daily life and may help improve their living conditions. The study highlights the processes and changes that were observed within these communities, and describes the optimum conditions required for implementation of ICT projects in poor environments.

This book is a synthesis of four case studies conducted in communities in rural and suburban areas of Kenya, Senegal, South Africa, and Uganda. In Kenya, the focus was on communities that had not yet been in contact with the new ICTs. The results suggest that these communities first needed training and information on ICTs and on the opportunities that ICTs could offer. The Ugandan case study looked at communities that were just starting to have contact with the new ICTs, and were beginning to perceive the possible uses of these tools in their areas of activity. In Senegal, the case study demonstrated that the people effectively use ICTs, notably in their daily activities and for personal purposes. Although the uses are more individualized in these communities, ICTs have also been appropriated and used for community purposes. The evaluation of the Msunduzi project in South Africa documented the relatively advanced use of a web site to support socio-economic development in the environment sector.

The book is divided into five chapters. Chapter 1, the introduction, describes the specific context of ICTs in the countries reviewed and analyses the general problems raised by ICTs in relation to development. It also addresses research problems and the conceptual framework for the study.

Chapter 2 gives an overview of the ICT environment in Kenya, Senegal, South Africa, and Uganda. It underscores the different institutional and regulatory changes that were implemented in these countries to develop the telecommunications infrastructure. It also shows that a consistent and systematic policy aimed at integrating ICTs in all aspects of the economic and social life of the communities is unavailable. Nor is ICT infrastructure present in all regions of these countries. Most of the infrastructure and users are concentrated in the big cities, particularly in the capitals; whereas, the rural areas are neglected; thus creating a bipolarization of ICT usage.

Chapters 3 and 4 not only explore the expectations of African communities in using ICTs, but they also compare both the expected and observed impacts of ICTs within the communities studied in sub-Saharan Africa. Users noted some positive changes both in individual and collective activities and in their environment, thus attesting to the transforming potential of ICTs.

Chapter 5 highlights the major challenges in appropriating ICTs for development. It analyses lessons drawn from the various ICT projects to identify and draw attention to the main challenges in, and prospects for, the appropriation of ICTs by poor communities. These challenges concern decision-makers, researchers, development actors, and the communities themselves.

This study will be followed by a series of more systematic studies dealing with specific themes related to the hypotheses and problems generated during the research process.

Edith Adera
Team Leader
Acacia, IDRC

Alioune Camara
Senior Program Specialist
Acacia, IDRC

■ Acknowledgements

This book is the result of the collective and participatory work of a dynamic team endowed with diverse resources and skills. We thank all those who, through their expertise and dedication, contributed to this accomplishment, particularly the Acacia team as a whole. We also wish to thank particularly our IDRC colleagues: Alioune Camara, Bill Carman, Fred Carden, and Laurent Elder for their unfailing support as well as their significant intellectual and methodological contribution during the production of this document. We extend our thanks to Edith Adera, the team leader of the Acacia program, who spared no effort to carry through this assignment.

We are grateful to the African researchers who conducted the case studies in their respective countries with a great deal of professionalism. Our sincere thanks also go to the African communities that provided the information and participated actively in the validation of the findings reported in this book.

Lastly, we wish to express our deep appreciation to all IDRC staff in the Regional Office for Central and West Africa for their logistic and material support during the participatory workshops on the collection and validation of the evaluation results.

Ramata Molo Thioune
Knowledge Analyst
Acacia, IDRC

Chapter 1

Introduction

Questioning ICTs and development in Africa

For several years, many researchers have been showing particular interest in information and communication technologies (ICTs). According to the Committee on Science and Technology at the Service of Development, ICTs "will become crucially important for sustainable development in developing countries" (Credé and Mansell 1998: ix). For the past two decades, most developed countries have witnessed significant changes that can be traced to ICTs. These multidimensional changes (technical, financial and economic, cultural, social, and geo-political) have been observed in almost all aspects of life: economics; education; communications; leisure; and travel.

Furthermore, the changes observed in these countries have led to what is now referred to as "the knowledge society." ICTs have made it possible to find fast access to, and distribution of, information as well as new ways of doing business in real time at a cheaper cost. However, a considerable gap exists between developing countries, notably African countries, and developed ones in terms of the contribution of ICTs to the creation of wealth. The gap has tended to widen between developed countries, the technology suppliers, and the receiving developing countries. At the same time, the gap between the elites and the grassroots communities within these developing countries is also expanding in terms of their access to ICTs. If measures are not taken to make ICTs both affordable and easy to use, access to them will be insignificant in developing countries.

Many initiatives have been taken at the international level to support Africa's efforts to develop communication infrastructure and services that are connected to the world information highways. These efforts are designed to enable African countries to find faster ways to achieve durable and sustainable development. However, although most of the actors agree intuitively on the positive role that ICTs can play in the development process, the links between development and the use of ICTs are yet to be clearly established and rigorously supported by empirical results from Africa.

There is no doubt that ICTs play an important role in developed countries, but does the economic structure of these countries favour this role of ICTs in development? Davison et al. (2000) do think so. They state that in developed countries, the evolution of ICTs has been linked closely to the power and economic boom of these countries, and that there has been a strong positive correlation between development levels and the adoption of increasingly sophisticated and complex technologies.

Although the new (digital) technologies may be impressive, they cannot determine the changes expected from their uses. They are no more than catalysts that facilitate these changes. Like any other technology, it is the social context in which they have been introduced and implemented that determines their uses and impacts. The digital revolution is relevant for Africa only if it takes into consideration the daily realities and aspirations of individuals (Uimonen 1997).

Davison et al. (2000) went further by arguing that ICTs have, to a large extent, been developed in the context of, and for the cultural and social standards of, a few rich countries (Western Europe, North America, East and Southeast Asia, and Australia). These innovations can help meet market pressures but not the needs of the poor, who have very weak purchasing power (UNDP 2001).

Another idea developed by the International Telecommunications Union (1997) proposes that factors that strongly influence the introduction and spread of the Internet are wealth, telecommunications infrastructure (quality and number), the number of microcomputers, the relatively low cost of communications (telephone and Internet), language, education, and training. Yet, Africa is known for being a continent with one of the world lowest growth rates in all types of infrastructure.

In this book, we concur with UNDP (2001) that even if sustainable economic growth facilitates the creation and diffusion of useful innovations, technology is not only the result of growth but can be used to support growth and development. ICTs are credited with the ability to transform, and deep and significant changes are expected from their widespread use in Africa. From this standpoint African countries can take maximum advantage of the new technologies even if major challenges remain. These challenges include adapting ICTs to local conditions and uses in developing countries, and allowing each country to understand these innovations and adjust them to their own development needs.

Therefore, development in Africa depends on the continent's capacity to create wealth first to significantly reduce poverty and then to raise its capacity to create wealth to unprecedented and sustainable levels. The most optimistic observers estimate that with the era of new technologies and networks, African countries have an unprecedented opportunity to gain access to, to take advantage of, and most importantly, to contribute fully to this new world constructed on knowledge. Indeed, accurate and reliable information is a key element for sustainable development (Brodnig and Mayer-Schönberger 2000)

In June 1996, the United Nations Commission on Science and Technology for Development (UNCSTD) in collaboration with IDRC proposed five development indicators that focused on the improvement of the quality of life: education, health, income, governance, and technology (Credé and Mansell 1998). If we consider that these five indicators are key indicators of development for African countries, ICTs can be socially beneficial only if they contribute to: poverty eradication (higher income), improved health and education, better use and more equitable sharing of resources, and raising participation in the decision-making processes (and in this regard, access to information is crucial).

General framework

For the past few years, development actors have shown increasing interest in the role that ICTs can play in development. However, there was a blatant lack of empirical data (mainly quantitative information) to verify this link. The scientific community that was interested in these issues conducted many studies, but most of the research dealt with "macro" and "meso" levels. The "micro" aspects, those that the grassroots communities are specifically interested in, were not sufficiently studied and documented.

By documenting the research conducted by the Acacia program in Kenya, Senegal, South Africa, and Uganda, this book, which is a synthesis of many evaluation reports, tries to demonstrate the potential of ICTs for development in sub-Saharan Africa. It also identifies the major challenges that confront the communities involved in the process of appropriating ICTs for development. Its purpose is to share Acacia's experiences in the processes, resources, products and behaviours that were drawn from the research it supported with grassroots communities (individuals and organizations) in sub-Saharan Africa.

Methodology

The methodological approach used in this study was mainly participatory and iterative. It was inspired by the approach of the Acacia program and its ELSA component (see Appendix 1).

Background to the study

The study was prepared according to a participatory and iterative approach that necessitated consultation with different partners, researchers and development actors. In May 2000, at an ELSA meeting in Kampala, the need for this study was first expressed by IDRC representatives. Their concerns were summarized in the following question: What are the main lessons from the Acacia program and, more precisely, what are the impacts on the development of the targeted communities? In August 2000, a methodological workshop was held in Nairobi that brought together different Acacia partners who were drawn from various backgrounds, but who all shared an interest in ICTs. The purpose of the workshop was to agree on the evaluation methodology to be followed, given that this study would involve four countries (Kenya, Senegal, South Africa, and Uganda) and many researchers. An important output of this workshop was an evaluation matrix that was used to design the evaluation methodology and the quantitative and qualitative instruments for data collection. These tools were shared among all parties and adjusted according to regional differences. In September 2000, the study was launched in the four countries. A workshop was later organized in each of the countries to validate the evaluation results.

Evaluation problems and issues

Using a participatory approach and process, all participants identified evaluation issues at the methodological workshop held in Nairobi in August 2000. On the basis of the study objectives, the participants first identified major issues or themes for evaluation. Next, they determined the main issues to be researched, identified specific issues, and determined for each issue the relevant information to be collected, the information sources, and the appropriate methods of data collection. The main evaluation issues that were identified were:

1. Economic, technical, political and social environments in which ICTs have been introduced.
2. Community access to ICTs.
3. Community involvement in the process of introducing ICTs.
4. Community responses to ICTs.
5. Technologies introduced.
6. Applications and content developed along with the introduction of ICTs.
7. Impacts of ICT introduction and use by the communities.
8. Capacity building among different groups.

Methods and instruments of data collection

This study analyses the content of various regional reports. For the preparation of these regional reports, data collection was done using the methods identified at the Nairobi workshop. The IDRC research and evaluation team in Dakar adapted the most appropriate methods, and as a result, identified the most suitable data collection methods. A range of data collection tools and instruments was then established. Quantitative methods were combined with qualitative ones. The choice between methods was determined by the nature of questions to be answered and, hence, the data to be collected. Questionnaires were chosen as the instruments for quantitative data collection, and (individual or group) conversation guides were the preferred method for secondary qualitative information.

The following conversation guides, targeting specific categories of respondents, were drawn up and used:

1. Information and communication infrastructure map designed for community representatives.
2. Social map designed for the same target.
3. Conversation guide designed for specific groups (e.g., women and young people).
4. Conversation guide designed for community organizations (e.g., GPF, SCA, and corporate bodies).
5. Conversation guide designed for technicians, specialists, and consultants.

6. Documentary analysis guide indicating all the documents that might interest the research team.

These data collection instruments were then translated into English and sent to colleagues in the other IDRC regional offices (South Africa and Kenya) involved in this study. Given that the contexts were different, it was up to each regional office to adapt the instruments to local conditions.

Sampling

The unit of analysis is the communities benefiting from Acacia projects. In the reports used in this study, the projects constituted the program gateways into these communities; therefore, sampling was done on the basis of these projects. At the Nairobi workshop, a number of criteria were defined for project selection and for the sites to be included in the study. Stratification was chosen as the sampling method. First, projects were selected, then sites to be studied are chosen within these projects and in each of the sites, a sample of respondents was selected. The following criteria were agreed upon at the Nairobi workshop for project selection:

*   Project maturity: more than one year of operation.
*   Geographic location: rural, suburban, and urban areas.

The application of these criteria resulted in the following stratified sampling:

*   Strata 1: project selection.
*   Strata 2: site selection.
*   Strata 3: respondent selection.

Based on this sampling, four projects were selected in Senegal, one in (Kenya), and two in Uganda. A project developed and implemented in South Africa was also included to help obtain a broader vision and to compare different aspects of the program.

Data collection and processing

Data were collected using a participatory approach. Qualitative data collection required interviews with groups and individuals. Quantitative data were collected using questionnaires. Given the objectives of the study, we classified respondents into two groups: users and non-users, and within each of these sub-groups, they were chosen randomly. Secondary data were obtained from community telecentres (e.g., statistics on users, types of requested services, and frequency of service use). Quantitative data were processed with statistical software (SPSS in Senegal and Kenya, EPI-INFO in Uganda); whereas, qualitative data were analysed using the content analysis method.

Methodological limitations

The Nairobi methodological workshop had identified clear and relevant questions that would evaluate the process and impacts of introducing ICTs in the communities. One of the major difficulties encountered in this study was the differing maturity of the selected projects. Initially, it was agreed to conduct this study in Kenya plus the four countries where Acacia was concentrated (Mozambique, Senegal, South Africa, and Uganda). This selection was to include a fairly varied range of projects that were mature enough to provide answers to the questions raised by the evaluation. But only the four projects in Senegal had been active for 2 years. In Uganda and Kenya, the projects had only been in operation for a year and ICTs had not yet been introduced (at the time of data collection). The immediate consequence of this was that not all of the research questions could be answered and some of those that were answered were only partially answered. In addition, the research was exploratory and descriptive, and little concern was given to ensuring that the sample chosen was statistically meaningful. Therefore, the results should be read with caution.

Summary of projects

Senegal

Youth cyber spaces in intermediate and secondary education in Senegal (project number 065256, implemented by the Groupe d'études et d'enseignement de la population (GEEP)). GEEP is trying to sensitize Senegalese authorities to the need to include sex education and environmental issues in school syllabuses. GEEP has set up Family Life Education (FLE) clubs in some schools to help fill this gap in the curriculum. However, these clubs are located far away from the main information centres and do not work often together. The youth cyber space project experimented with the introduction of ICTs into the network of FLE clubs to allow both for more frequent communication and for improved information flow. More specifically, this experiment attempted to improve the learning, facilitation, and sensitization model used by the FLE clubs to promote population, environment, and sustainable development issues. ICTs were introduced through the creation of youth cyber spaces (point of access to ICTs) in secondary education in Senegal.

Use and appropriation of ICTs by community organizations in Senegal (project number 065198, in collaboration with ENDA and local community organizations). This project was aimed at strengthening local participation in suburban and marginalized areas and districts of Dakar. A research-action methodology, which also included training, was implemented to enable the organizations concerned to use ICTs in ways that would encourage the development of sustainable patterns of ICT use through a network of community resource centres that were managed by the communities themselves.

Introduction of ICTs to the Management and Rehabilitation of Village Communities (project number 065226, in collaboration with the West Africa Rural Foundation (WARF)). This project was implemented in three rural communities located in the Tambacounda region of Senegal. It was prompted by the observation that community leaders living far away from the capital were called upon to take important decisions (e.g., formulating local development plans and negotiating with strategic partners), given the government's commitment to decentralization and decision-making by local authorities. However, most of the information needed for these decisions was disparate when available. The project aimed at taking actions that would favour the use of ICTs by different actors. It also sought to assess the impacts of ICTs on resource management and on economic and community education activities while investigating the factors influencing the acceptability and appropriation of these innovations.

ICTs and Decentralization of Trade Point Senegal (project number 065211, in partnership with Trade Point Senegal). This project was implemented in six communities in Senegal to demonstrate that ICTs could provide economic units with the same access to sources of information, and thus enabled them to improve the decisions they make regarding activities and businesses. More precisely, the idea was to experiment with the provision of the services offered by Trade Point Senegal to economic actors doing business in locations outside Dakar (the capital). ICTs were provided through a network of community structures located at different community levels in two regions of the country (Saint-Louis and Thiès).

Kenya

Enhancing women's participation in governance through increased access to civic information (project number 055394, with the Family Support Institute). The main objective of this project was to develop the existing infrastructure at community documentation centres. These centres were the points of access to ICT resources (notably the Internet), which were used to provide information to the women of the Kakamega and Makueni rural communities and to promote their participation in governance. More precisely, the project tried to demonstrate that ICTs, when combined with traditional information systems and networks, allowed women to access civic information to develop their capacities to participate in political decision-making bodies, and in particular, in decisions concerning women's issues.

Uganda

Economic empowerment of women through ICTs in Uganda (project number 055449, carried out by the Council for the Economic Empowerment of Women of Africa). This project mainly intended to demonstrate how ICTs could enable female workers and women's organizations involved in the promotion of entrepreneurship to find ways in which women could be better involved in the economic life of the community.

African Highlands Initiative (project number 055297). The African Highlands Initiative (AHI) is a collaborative research program focusing on natural resource management in the highlands of East and Central Africa. Its ambition was to promote community development and the sustainable use of natural resources in the East and Central African highlands, an area of intensive agriculture. The objectives were to help farmers to enhance their knowledge and understanding of the technological choices that they had to make, to improve their decision-making capacity, take advantage of the increasing opportunities available for marketing their production, and benefit from training in natural resource management.

South Africa

The Msunduzi community network project (project number 003981). This project was inspired by the belief that environment and development initiatives in the Pietermaritzburg area might be reinforced by enhancing the ICT capacities of local community organizations that were collaborating with the same NGO. The overall objective was to improve the environment around the Msunduzi River. The project was designed to facilitate access to ICTs by organizations and communities to improve their decision-making capacity. An efficient community model of electronic information and communication was established with points of access to link communities to an ICT network.

Conceptual framework

By questioning the concept of community development, the definition of ICTs and the contributions of ICTs to the development process, this book has been able to look closely at the issues surrounding community development. Below is a brief summary of the concepts and terms used in the study.

Community development

The use of ICTs is expected to bring about a change in the behaviour of the individuals and groups who make up the communities. Community development can be defined as a global, dynamic, iterative, and interactive process of change that constitutes the source of significant and measurable improvements in various aspects of life and provides some degree of satisfaction. In this specific context, we mean the sustainable satisfaction of basic needs, for example, in education, health, employment and entrepreneurship, natural resource management, and governance through the use of ICTs. Community development concerns individuals and organizations or institutions and their inter-relationships and inter-connectedness. It implies the participation of all community components in this process. It also implies capacity building in order to favour the creation of the conditions required for an increase in necessary resources.

Community

The term 'community' here designates both the individuals and their communities, and organizations or associations that have access to ICTs or are potential users of ICTs. It does not matter whether they are women's organizations, youth associations, trade organizations in the informal sector, or groupings of arts and crafts workers and farmers.

Participation

The use of ICTs for community development implies the participation of all components of a given community. Participation is understood in many ways but in this document it refers to an organized effort accomplished by the members themselves with a view to achieving the development objectives that they had assigned to themselves (Ziliotto 1989). Community participation is seen in this context as a process that creates the conditions required to speed up changes induced by, and expected from, ICTs.

Information and Communication Technologies (ICTs)

Even if ICTs – mainly the new ICTs – often make us think of the Internet, they refer to the possibilities offered by the convergence of data processing techniques, electronic media, and telecommunications, a convergence that has become evident over the past few years. ICTs do not exclude traditional services such as radio and television, which can be broadcast through the same digital medium as the other services.

In this study, ICTs are grouped under two categories: 'traditional' and 'new'. Traditional ICTs are radio, television, fixed line telephones, and facsimile machines, which have been gradually ingrained in the daily habits and lives of people and communities. The 'new' ICTs consist of computers and specific data processing applications accessible through those computers (email, Internet, word processing, and other data processing applications). Although cellular phones and, more generally, wireless technologies, might be included in this category, they are not covered by this study.

Impacts

Given the transforming capacity ascribed to ICTs, their use is expected to produce more or less significant impacts. This impact should be understood here as changes in behaviours, relations, activities, or intervention strategies that are influenced by projects which introduce ICTs to communities. These changes are expected to contribute to the achievement of a better quality of life for the population or communities.

Access

Expected changes would be dependent on access to ICTs. Access should be understood in this study to mean the opportunity to use ICTs (e.g., availability, financial capacity, and technical capacity).

Chapter 2

The context of ICTs in Africa: The cases of Kenya, Senegal, South Africa, and Uganda

New ICTs are now found on the development agenda of African countries, and strategies have been gradually implemented to integrate them into the development process. Many countries have initiated significant reforms in the telecommunications sector: privatizing companies, liberalizing and ending national monopolies in the sector. However, most countries do not appear to have an integrated vision of the policies implemented in this sector. The reforms introduced are still sectoral in nature, and the corollary of this vision is that an integrated approach, which would be more holistic in terms of policies designed to introduce and to appropriate ICTs for development, has not yet been adopted.

This chapter gives an overview of the institutional context of ICTs in four countries: Kenya, Senegal, South Africa, and Uganda. The findings presented in this study were obtained from projects executed in these countries. The analysis of the institutional framework revealed that these countries have been gradually developing regulatory frameworks and structures designed to promote new ICTs. However, the situations appear to vary from one country to another depending on the state of infrastructure, level of information that decision-makers have on ICTs, and the capacity of the country to attract foreign investments.

South Africa

South Africa is described as a leading country in telecommunications in Africa because it possesses 40% of all telephone lines on the continent. Like in most African countries, the level of growth in its telecommunications sector is linked to the significant changes in the institutional environment governing the sector. Since the enforcement of the Communication Act in 1996, there has been rapid growth in the telecom sector, which is still dominated by the State. Telkom Ltd., the once completely state-owned company, holds a *de facto* monopoly on fixed line telephone services. This monopoly was scheduled to end in May 2002. Continued development of this sector poses numerous challenges in South Africa, particularly for its fixed line operator, Telkom Ltd. Moreover, the sector is under growing pressure to meet the demand of the millions of South Africans who still do not have access to basic telecommunication services.

In March 1997, the State sold 30% of its shares to strategic partners most of whom are foreigners (United States Department of Commerce 1999). The sale yielded USD1.2 billion, which constituted the largest direct foreign investment ever in infrastructure development in South Africa. Partnership with the private sector enabled the country to extend coverage of its telephone network to new areas, to modernize the network, and to provide consumers with state-of-the-art services. Telkom's ambition with this strategy was to prepare for the inevitable competition and to meet the needs of an increasingly demanding customer. In this connection, Telkom launched a far-reaching network extension program with the creation of over 3 million additional lines (a 75% increase) between 1997 and 1999. In 2001, the number of fixed lines was estimated at 5,860,000 (Table 1).

In early 2000, the South African Telecommunications Regulation Agency (SATRA) and the Independent Broadcasting Authority (IBA) were merged into an independent entity called the Independent Communications Authority of South Africa (ICASA). ICASA was charged with regulating communications (structures and technologies) at the national level. The purpose of this merger was to clarify the situation in the telecommunications sector, which had been characterized by confusion due to the decentralization of decision-making centres.

Table 1: A few telecommunications indicators (South Africa)

Indicator	2000	2001
Fixed telephone lines	5,492,838	5,860,000*
Cellular subscribers	6,000,000	9,000,000
Teledensity (%)	11.2	12.2
Public telephones	173,064	—
Fixed telephone operators	1	1
Cellular telephone operators	2	3
Internet subscribers	370,000	2,853,453

Source: BMI-TechKnowledge, *Communications Technologies Handbook 2001* (2001).

Note: *Estimate.

This had caused a lack of clarity in the responsibilities of each agency (SATRA and IBA). The new agency reflected the desire for more consistency in the evolution of the telecommunications sector (technology convergence and higher number of operators). With the continuing evolution in the telecommunications sector, a second fixed line telephone operator is expected to arrive on the market when Telkom's monopoly ends in May 2002.

The cellular phone industry also recorded unprecedented growth in the country. Up to October 1997, there were 1.4 million cellular phone subscribers. One of the conditions imposed on cellular phone license holders then (Vodacom and MTN) was to invest also in community projects aimed at promoting universal access to telecommunication services at the national level. For example, Vodacom was to allocate, over a 4-year period, 22,000 lines in underprivileged areas; whereas, MTN was to create 7,500 points of access across the country. In addition, a third operating license was granted to a consortium of private cellular phone operators made up of groups of local business traders and a foreign partner. The number of subscribers to cellular telephony was estimated at 9 million in 2001 (Table 1). Typical costs for fixed line and cellular telephones are given in Table 2.

Table 2: Telecommunication service rates in South Africa
(in ZAR per minute)

Operator	Services	Costs (Tax Included)
Telkom (fixed)	Local Calls	0.02
	0–50 km	0.13
	50–100 km	0.50
	>100 km	1.02
Vodacom (Cellular)	Access to network	95.00 per year
	From a cellular phone to another (within the Vodacom Network)	1.60 peak 0.75 off-peak
MTN (Cellular)	Local and national	1.60 peak 0.75 off-peak
	From a cellular phone to another (within the MTN Network)	1.66 peak 0.75 off-peak
	Cell phone call (from MTN Network to another)	1.87 peak 0.75 off-peak

Source: BMI-TechKnowledge (2001).

The information technology economy also witnessed considerable growth. Between 1997 and 1999, the share of information technologies increased by almost 12.5% annually. Between high value-added and high-yield sectors (such as network development and service and data integration systems), and low-yield sectors (such as computer manufacturing and distributing outfits), there are real opportunities in the information technology market.

Therefore, small- and medium-sized enterprises are gradually becoming the levers of this information economy. These enterprises are putting in place strategies to exploit the potential that exists in the telecommunications sector through the convergence of technology that favours both direct and indirect employment generation. The main trends in the information economy in South Africa are: the emergence of an economy increasingly based on the Internet; the development of e-commerce; and technologies of media convergence.

Kenya

In Kenya, the institutional framework of the telecommunications sector is still dominated by the State. However, the situation changed considerably with the promulgation of the 1998 Telecommunications Law, which became effective on 1 July 1999 and replaced the law governing the Kenya Post and Telecommunications Company. It provided for the institution of an independent organization, the Communications Commission of Kenya (CCK) to regulate all aspects of the sector, including: licensing, price regulation, defining equipment standards, managing radio frequencies and inter-connections, and ensuring compliance with general service obligations. The 1998 law also provided for the establishment of a National Communications Secretariat (NCS), lodged with the Ministry of Information and Telecommunication. The role of NCS is to advise the State on policies in the information and telecommunications sector.

Telkom Kenya Limited (TKL), which used to be part of the Kenya Post and Telecommunications Company (KPTC), is now one of the many structures set up to manage the networks. It was established in 1999 when KPTC was split into three distinct legal entities: TKL, PCK (Postal Corporation of Kenya), and CCK. TKL manages all activities related to telecommunications and PCK controls the licenses and runs the services previously provided by KPTC. Although TKL is now facing competition from newcomers in other sectors where it holds no monopoly, following market liberalization, it still seems to have some advantage over the others as a public telecommunications operator.

Following liberalization of the non-strategic telecommunications subsectors and the opening of value-added services in 1991, the number of private providers of telecommunication services increased considerably. There are now over 350 enterprises specializing in the sale, installation, maintenance, and wiring of telephone hardware. Recent statistics available (June 2001) indicate that there are about 60 Internet and other related services providers in the country.

The development of the telecommunications infrastructure in Kenya was relatively fast. The country's telephone capacity has increased from 112,861 lines in 1981 to almost 400,000 lines in 2000. The average annual growth rate of telephone communications rose from 16.6% in 1981 to 24.3% in 1990, but fell to 15% later in 1997. Public telephone services recorded a spectacular development over this period, with public telephone boxes rising from 588 in 1981 to about 7,500 in 2001. The cellular phone market is now distributed between two private providers: Safaricom and Kencell Communications Limited (KCL). These two cellular operators had a total of about 200,000 subscribers in 2001 (Table 3).

Teledensity is about 0.16 fixed lines per hundred inhabitants in the rural area and 4 fixed lines per hundred inhabitants in the urban area. In terms of market penetration, about 4.2% of country households own a telephone line. However, this rate varies considerably: it is 0.1% in remote areas compared with 27.7% for the city of Nairobi. Most of the telephones available in urban areas belong to offices and not households. Typical costs for fixed and cellular telephones are given in Table 4.

Table 3: A few telecommunication indicators (Kenya)

Indicator	2000	2001
Fixed telephone lines	310,000	400,000*
Cellular subscribers	60,000	200,000
Teledensity (%)	1.0	1.2
Public telephones	7,084	7,500
Fixed telephone operators	1	1
Cellular telephone operators	2	2
Internet subscribers	55,000	75,000

Source: BMI-TechKnowledge (2001).

Note: *Estimate.

Table 4: Telecommunication service rates in Kenya (2002)

Operator	Service	Costs (USD)
Telkom Kenya Ltd (fixed)	Access to network	39.00
	Monthly fixed charge	3.28
	Local call/3 minutes	0.06
	National inter-urban calls (150 km)/minute	0.21
	International calls to USA/minute	2.20
	International link at 64kbps/month	8200.00
Safaricom Kenya Ltd (Pre-paid phone card)	Access to network	32.00
	From a cellular phone to another (within Safaricom Network)/minute	0.19
	Cellular phone (from Safaricom Network to another) /minute	0.31
	From a cellular phone to a fixed phone/minute	0.31
Kencell Commun. Ltd (Pre-paid phone card)	Access to network	37.00
	From a cellular phone to another (within Kencell Network)/minute	0.19
	Cellular phone (from Kencell Network to another)/minute	0.51
	From a cellular phone to a fixed phone/minute	0.32

Source: BMI-TechKnowledge (2001).

Uganda

In Uganda, the technological environment has also witnessed considerable growth as a result of changes at the global level – advances in information and communication technologies – and especially by local dynamics – such as the liberalization of the communication sector, which attracted private investments. Since the 1990s, there are more than 20 private FM radio stations in Uganda. Most of them can be received in and around Kampala, the capital, and in other big cities like Mbarara, Gulu, Kabale, and Soroti. According to the World Bank (1999) there were 126 radio receivers for every 1,000 inhabitants in 1996. With the opening of many FM radio stations, the number of radio receivers increased considerably. The area covered by all these stations is often very limited. Although the National Radio Broadcast (Radio Uganda) covers in principle the entire country, reception quality is poor. According to Achia (2000), Radio Uganda covers only 50% of the country. Other media such as television cover an even more limited area.

With Uganda Telecom Limited (UTL), most of the big cities in the country are connected to telephone networks. According to Kibombo and Kayambwe (2000), Uganda Post and Telecommunications, the single telephone operator in the country until 1997, had only 50,829 subscribers at the end of 2002. As Achia (2000) pointed out, the number of subscribers increased considerably as three new cellular phone operators arrived on the market (Celtel, MTN Uganda, and Mango, an affiliate of UTL). In July 2000, the country had over 60,000 fixed telephone lines and 122,000 subscribers to cellular phone services. Teledensity is estimated at about 0.85% Achia (2000), reflecting roughly a 300% increase over the past four years (Table 5).

Despite the fact that the area covered by the telephone network is expanding and that there is a considerable increase in the number of subscribers, the use of new ICTs such as the Internet and email is still very limited. As Achia (2000) observed, Internet and email started late in Uganda, the first batch of connections to the Internet was made during the Great Lakes crisis (1994–1996). In 2001, there was more than ten Internet service providers (ISPs) for a total of over 25,000 users, mainly through cyber-cafés in Kampala and some other cities of the country. Typical costs for telephones and cellular telephones are given in Table 6.

Table 5: A few telecommunications indicators (Uganda)

Indicator	2000	2001
Fixed telephone lines	60,000	100,000*
Cellular subscribers	120,000	-
Teledensity (%)	0.85	1
Public telephones	3,600	5,000
Fixed telephone operators	1	1
Cellular telephone operators	3	3
Internet subscribers	15,000	25,000

Source: BMI-TechKnowledge (2001).
Note: * Estimate

The few television stations found in the country (about six) are all based in Kampala. Not all of them are operational, and those that are functional only cover Kampala and its outskirts. The World Bank (1999) estimates that there were 26 television sets per 1,000 inhabitants in 1997.

Senegal

In Senegal, like in most African countries, the telecommunications environment has evolved considerably. Thanks to the existence of a relatively modern infrastructure that covers a large part of the country, the technological environment is favourable to the introduction of ICTs. Senegal quickly implemented a strategy for introducing ICTs in the country through the national telephone company, SONATEL. The network for data transmission (Senpac), launched in 1988, gave enterprises access to data banks and allowed them to make connect to foreign networks at a speed of up to 19,200 bps. Since 1997, the speed has increased to 64 kbps on the national and international lines, and the network is entirely digital.

The 30 departments (administrative subdivisions) of the country are connected to the central network through a digital transmission link, and all administrative centres in rural communities have access to telephones.

Table 6: Telecommunications service rates in Uganda (2000)

Operator	Services	Costs (USD)
Uganda Telecom Ltd (fixed line)	Access to network	11.33
	Monthly fixed charge	0.66
	Local calls/ 3 minutes	0.50
	National inter-urban calls (150 km)/minute	1.33
	International calls (to USA)/minute	1.53
MTN Uganda Ltd (Pre-paid phone card)	Access to network	25.57
	Monthly fixed charge	19.77
	Local calls/3 minutes	0.12
	National inter-urban calls/minute	0.14
	International calls to USA/minute	0.85
Celtel (Pre-paid phone card)	Access to network	28.00
	Monthly fixed charge	10.00
	From a cellular phone to another (within Celtel Network) /minute	0.23
	From a cell phone (from Kencell Network to another) /minute	0.23
	From a cell phone to a fixed phone/minute	0.32
	International calls (to USA)/minute	1.70

Source: BMI-TechKnowledge (2001).

Twenty-two of the thirty departments are connected to the central network by fibre optic cables. SONATEL has laid 2000 km of fibre optic cables across the country. In addition, 24 departments have access to an Integrated Services Digital Network (ISDN), and specialized international digital links at 64 kbps through satellite are possible. A digital cellular network (GSM standard) implemented by SONATEL (Alizé) and its competitor SENTEL, covers the country's main cities and road network, and is interconnected with foreign networks (e.g., Spain, Great Britain, and Italy).

The country has fourteen Internet service providers (ISPs). Twelve of these are based in Dakar and the other two in Saint-Louis and Ziguinchor. About 50 organizations are connected to the Internet through a specialized link to SONATEL, and the Senegal National Internet Centre (NIC) has registered 400 domain names. Since April 1999, an Internet Protocol network (IP), Sentranet, which is based on 155 mbps, 34 mbps and 2 mbps links, connects all the country's main cities and towns and allows the implementation of intranet and extranet services. A first license for satellite communication was delivered to Iridium, a US-based company which officially launched its activities in Senegal in early October 1999.

The number of telephone lines increased from 81,000 in 1998 to 200,000 in December 2000 (more than 100% between 1998 and 2000), then to 230,000 in May 2001. This corresponds to an urban teledensity of about 2.54% and a rural teledensity of 0.05%. The number of fixed telephone lines rose to 280,000 in July 2002 (OSIRIS 2002) (Table 7). However, telephone lines are not evenly distributed across the country. About 64% of the lines are concentrated in Dakar. The region of Thiès has 14,043 telephone lines, or 5% of the national network. Telephone service covers the entire region of Saint-Louis down to the rural districts and to few rural communities with 14,539 lines.

In November 2000, statistics provided by SONATEL indicated that 12,492 telephone centres were operating in Senegal. The 1999 census reported that about 20 cyber-cafés and 80 telephone centres were connected to the Internet. OSIRIS (2002) reported that there were 11,000 Internet subscribers in February 2001. In May 2001, there were 48 private and 104 public ISPs, with 56% of these in Dakar (Table 8). When the international bandwidth speed increases to 54 mbps (May 2002), Internet use is expected to grow.

Table 7: A few telecommunication Indicators (Senegal)

Fixed telephone lines	280,000 (April 2002)
Cellular subscribers	550,000 (July 2002)
Fixed telephone operators	1
Cellular telephone operators	2
International bandwidth	54 mbps
ISPs	14
Internet subscribers	About 11,000 (February 2001)
.sn registered domains	672 (May 2001)
Sites actually online	160 (May 2001)
Internet access points	>150
Customs duties payable on computers	Customs duties 0+ 5% customs stamp
VAT payable on computers	18%
VAT payable on communications	18%

Source: OSIRIS (2002).

Following the application of law number 98-36 (17 April 1998), computer hardware and telematic equipment were exempted from customs duties. However, peripherals (e.g., printers, scanners, and CD-ROM drives) and electric equipment were liable to a 55% tax. In addition, locally manufactured capital goods for data processing and telematic equipment were subject to a 25% tax.

The sector benefited from heavy investments from the 1980s onward. The annual average investment amounted to 18 billion FCFA. The sector contributed directly, in 1996, to raising the GDP by 2.6%, and as a support to production, it had a positive effect on all other national economic activities. It also contributed to employment generation: 10,000 jobs were created between 1992 and 1998, especially within telecentres.

For its Internet related services, SONATEL applies "all taxes included" (ATI) rates to its customers:

- Connecting to the network costs 30,000 FCFA.
- Monthly subscription with unlimited Internet connection is 10,000 FCFA.
- Telephone connection (local rate) is set at 60 FCFA for every 2 minutes at peak periods and every 4 minutes at off-peak periods.

SONATEL is gradually developing products targeted at specific users. This is how the flat rate Internet service charge was launched in May 2002. It allows a customer to benefit from 10 hours of connection per month regardless of connection time at a monthly subscription cost of 10,000 FCFA (ATI). The fixed charge per hour is therefore 1,000 FCFA (ATI). With this service, SONATEL plans to attract more Internet users, while allowing them more surfing time. This service is targeted at Internet users who surf during daytime, professionals wishing to download large documents, and students.

Not everyone has access to telecommunication services due to the underdeveloped infrastructure in rural areas and to the low-purchasing power of some segments of the populations. It is important to note, however, that in almost all village communities, there is a communal use of the telephone even when it is privately owned. Family linkages and community life are such that an individual who cannot afford a household telephone line can receive telephone calls elsewhere in the communal. SONATEL is the major operator in the telecommunication sector. It has the monopoly in the fixed lines network. SONATEL is also the first operator, followed by SENTEL, in the GSM network. Apart from these two major Internet service providers, namely SONATEL (Telecomplus) and SENTEL, there are about ten other service providers.

Despite some progress in infrastructure development and rates, Senegal has not yet developed a systematic policy on ICTs. Only a few initiatives by the State, SONATEL, NGOs, and some development institutions have been reported. The State has not yet put in place a consistent policy framework to integrate new ICTs into the overall macro-economic framework.

Table 8: Private and public Internet Service Providers in Senegal

Private	Public
Métissacana	UCAD
AFRICANET	AUPELF-UREF
ENDA	Prime Minister's Office
Arc Informatique	Gaston Berger University
Cyber Business Centre	Trade Point Senegal (TPS)
Point Net	
WAIT	
Zentel	
Sud Informatique	

Source: OSIRIS (2002).

Conclusion

It appears that the contexts and institutional frameworks within these countries are changing rapidly, which reflects their commitment to the information society. Many reforms have been introduced and measures have been taken by policy makers and telecommunication operators. Despite these reforms, telecommunication costs are still relatively high, particularly in the provinces; whereas, international communications costs are relatively cheaper. This is evidence that telecommunication policies still favour international rather than national communications. Furthermore, although the foundations of integration into the information society have been laid, integration into the information economy remains the responsibility of the policy makers and the different development actors. In fact, in these countries, a systematic and consistent policy to integrate ICTs into all aspects of economic and social life is yet to be formulated. The development of the telecommunication sector is far from being integrated into the overall macro-economic framework. The economic fabric of these countries continues to reflect a sectoral approach to telecommunication policy.

Chapter 3

Information and Communication Technologies: Expectations of African communities

One of the major development challenges confronting Africa is to develop the capacities, strategies, and mechanisms necessary to take full advantage of the opportunities offered by ICTs for development. Given the potential for ICTs to induce changes, many development analysts believe that these instruments can play an important role in the development process. In Africa, development theorists anticipate significant changes, particularly within the fabric of communities. These expectations are generally based only on changes observed in economically more advanced (usually Western) societies, but are not generally supported by facts.

The purpose of this chapter is to demonstrate what African communities expect from ICTs. Examples are given of attempts to introduce and use ICTs in African communities. The effects or changes that actual and potential users of ICTs expect to see in their own communities are described. In addition, community views on the anticipated usefulness of ICTs for improving their living conditions are discussed. This chapter synthesizes the observations reported in several research-action projects supported by Acacia in Kenya, Senegal, South Africa, and Uganda. These projects were centred on concrete uses and applications of ICTs in community development rather than on connectivity.

Expectations expressed by individuals

Information and Communication Technologies (ICTs) give rise to many expectations among the communities surveyed. The hope suggests that an awareness of the role that ICT instruments can play in economic and social development is emerging. The effects or changes that individuals expect from ICTs are quite varied (Figure 1). In general, individuals plan to apply ICTs to their main areas of activity for their own development. As a rule, users (actual or potential) expect the use of ICTs to make positive changes in their jobs, education, health, agriculture, and environment. In communities that the Acacia-supported projects studied, the inhabitants were mostly active in agriculture, small businesses, and the service sector, and the effects they expected from ICTs revolved mainly around these activities.

Production activities

Information and Communication Technologies (ICTs) should facilitate business development through improved access to information on product prices (inputs and outputs), on markets, and on various other resources. Therefore, in agriculture, African farmers expect ICTs to facilitate access to: high-yielding varieties at competitive prices; input suppliers; credit institutions; and information on how to improve their farming practices to increase yield. For example, farmers in the Ross Béthio region of Senegal expect ICTs to provide access to new knowledge on irrigation techniques and rice varieties for irrigated farming because they would like to shift to cash crops, which earn better economic returns. In Uganda, although the people in Rubaya and the East and Central African highlands have not yet started to use the new ICTs, they hope to gain access to information and knowledge that would enable them to improve their agricultural production techniques and their income.

Trade

With regard to time management, ICTs can facilitate communication and reduce the time needed for transactions. This aspect is much talked about in the rural areas. In the main production areas, producers, in the absence of any information on prices and potential outlets (notably, on the local markets), are often at the mercy of intermediaries (who generally do not add any significant value to the production chain). The entrepreneurs using the services of Trade Point (TPS) in Senegal hope to meet new partners with whom they could set up large-scale farming and gain new markets for their produce. This would help them overcome constraints related to the narrowness of the local market in their farming area. Women entrepreneurs in the Buwama and Kampala regions of Uganda hoped that ICTs would give them access to information that would help them improve the financial position of their businesses (Table 9) (CEEWA 2001).

Table 9: Potential role of ICTs according to women entrepreneurs in Uganda

Perception	Percentage
Time saving	15.9
Search for outlets	14.5
Information on trade	14.5
Communication with suppliers and customers	40.7
Cost savings	4.3
No answer	10.1
Total	100.0

Source: 'Consolidated report on monitoring women entrepreneurs in the CEEWA project sites (Nabweru, Buwama, and Kampala),' May 2001.

Education and research

In education, students and teachers expected ICTs to improve their learning and teaching methods. They also hoped that they would have access to information that would help them enhance their classes and facilitate preparations for school exams. ICTs can boost research and assist in acquiring new knowledge. In Senegal, this potential raised great expectations among the educationists, and agriculture extension service workers, who settled in the rural areas to train farmers for companies such as SAED in Saint-Louis. So far, ICTs have not been used much as a way of acquiring new knowledge. The inadequacy of local content and limited access to ICTs constitute very serious problems.

Health

ICTs should make it possible to have access to information that would help improve preventive health education. This expectation is anticipated by health workers, notably in the region of Tambacounda in Senegal, which are land-locked and are often affected by recurrent epidemics of flu, malaria, and diarrhoea. The use of a computer warning system based on systematic data collection might be able to sharply reduce both mother and child mortality rates.

Social communication

As a facilitator of communication, ICTs could be able to contribute to bringing scattered members of the same family closer together (the creation and maintenance of a virtual community). This important effect is expected most notably in Uganda (Table 10). In land-locked regions like Podor and Matam in Senegal, known for their high migration levels, the inhabitants believe that ICTs (email and telephone) can contribute to minimizing transport costs, facilitating communication, and improving social life. This aspect is very important in the specific case of poor communities with relatively low incomes and high communication needs.

Women

Women seem to be less able to express the effects they want from ICTs. The majority feel that these "instruments are not made for them." This situation posed a problem within the Acacia program because women (along with youth) constituted one of the main target groups. A few women surveyed in Senegal seek information related to health, land ownership, and easy access to credit (Table 11).

Youth

Young people were very active in cultural and sports associations and most of them expressed the need to have access to support structures for their association. For example, they were looking for ways to reinforce their capacity for intervention and to obtain information on ways to cooperate with other groups. Students wanted access to pedagogic resources and

30

information on scholarships, school exams, competitions, and vocational opportunities.

Figure 1: Potential uses of ICTs by individuals in Uganda

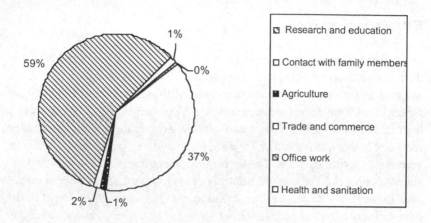

Source: Etta et al., 'Inquiries and questionnaires, ICTs and Community Development Study, Uganda, November 2000,' (2001).

Expectations of community organizations

Apart from the effects expected at the individual level, community organizations also had their own expectations.

Facilitating communication

In Uganda and Kenya, community organizations would use ICTs to facilitate communication processes and to mobilize their members through the esta-blishment of reliable, real-time communication systems, combining email, in particular, with traditional community communication systems. These organizations also expect the use of ICTs to improve management and to facilitate planning and organization of their activities. For community organizations, access to useful and relevant information for their members (e.g., economic, cultural, and sports activities) constituted a major concern. This information would be used to help members make better and more rapid decisions in their various activities. Generally, ICTs can improve the capacities of grassroots organizations to communicate and make their voices heard through the roles they play in their communities.

Establishing networks

Information and Communication Technologies (ICTs) can be used as a medium to establish networks between community members or with the outside world to improve the institutional context of these communities. In South Africa, in the rural communities around the Msunduzi River, ICTs, particularly Internet technologies, are expected to allow access to new communication tools and to provide a medium for discussion and exchange among different community organizations. These organizations expect to enhance their knowledge about the environment and development. These communities also expect ICTs to lead to the creation of new organizations and to the development of active partnerships between these organizations and other institutions. They also hope to influence development policies and encourage the changes needed to ensure improved natural resource management in areas surrounding the Msunduzi River, which are increasingly affected by ecological problems. In Senegal, ICTs are considered as development tools to facilitate access to information and to make recent information available to expand the knowledge base of local populations.

Establishing modern communication systems

Community organizations expect ICTs to provide modern, reliable, and fast communication systems that can be combined with traditional community communication systems (e.g., weekly markets and traditional drum systems).

Improving working conditions

Recurrently, the populations expect ICTs to improve working conditions within community organizations, particularly through improved time and resource management. This is important to these organizations because most of the community actors are voluntary workers. In remote and land-locked regions (e.g., Podor and Tambacounda), ICTs are expected to reduce the isolating effects of distance and allow effective participation of scattered actors in community life.

Increasing external contacts and diversifying partners

Entrepreneurs expect to gain more external contacts and thus increase the prospects of diversification of their economic partners. ICTs are also expected to contribute to employment generation through the creation of new jobs. The project leader of the Acacia-supported project "Introduction of ICTs to the Management and Rehabilitation of Village Communities" believes that ICTs can have a significant effect on local governance:

> Community Information Centres (CIC) play an important role in local governance: the fact that forms from the Maka Coulibantang registry office are made available at the CIC saves the people about 5,000 FCFA in transportation costs. This is one direct effect on individuals. Eventually, secondary positive effects are expected on schooling levels, specifically among girls. The father of an average family in Maka can hardly spare 5,000 FCFA to pay for a registry office form while he is beset with survival problems. With the CIC he will pay only 200 FCFA. Another secondary effect to be expected is the collection of reliable statistics for use in drawing up local development plan. (Statement made by Abdou Fall, Acacia Project Team Leader, at the feedback workshop on ICTs and Community Development, Senegal, July 2001).

Conclusion

In general, community expectations directly correspond to the theoretical effects described in the literature on ICT. Tables 10 and 11 show that these effects are often inaccurate and general in nature. They reflect the level of understanding that communities have of the relationship between ICTs and the improvement of their living conditions.

The positive attitude of communities toward ICTs is also remarkable: very few respondents are concerned with the potential negative effects of ICTs. This attitude is very important and can be construed as an inclination to adopt ICTs, or at least as non-rejection of these tools by the communities. This attitude also suggests that the transforming potential of ICTs can be exploited to enhance development efforts.

With regard to how projects on the introduction of ICTs can be effective, the people suggest that there probably cannot be a single strategy. Basic studies that seek to highlight the diverse needs and expectations of people must be systematically conducted. Furthermore, these expressed expectations can be used as reference points for future investigations designed to measure specific changes over time due to the use of ICTs.

Table 10: Changes expected from use of ICTs according to context envisaged (Uganda)

Context	Changes expected	Percentage
1. Workplace	Easy communication	31.8
	Facilitating profit-yielding activities	13.6
	Facilitating exam/test preparations	9.1
2. Contact with family	Easy communication	14.3
members	Settling family problems	7.8
	Reducing transportation costs	7.8
	Improving and stimulating socialization	5.3
3. Trade and transactions	Easy communication	0.5
	Facilitating transactions	1.0
4. Research and education	Improvements	0.2
	Acquiring new knowledge	0.2
5. Health and sanitation	Information about disease prevention	1.3
6. Agriculture	Information on high-yielding varieties	1.3
7. No response		5.8
Total		100.0

Source: Etta et al., 'Inquiries and questionnaires, ICTs and Community Development Study, Uganda, November 2000' (2001).

Table 11: The roles that ICTs are expected to play within communities (Senegal)

Roles (more than one answer from each respondent)	Number	Percentage
Development tool	144	28.6
Easier access to information	53	10.5
Better working conditions	49	9.7
Acquiring better knowledge	47	9.3
Reducing distance constraints	33	6.6
Facilitator	32	6.4
Time saving (faster pace of activities and decision-making)	28	5.6
Increasing external contacts	18	3.6
Facilitating changes in the community	18	3.6
Favouring integration	16	3.2
Making recent information available	12	2.4
Creation of new jobs	15	3.0
Combating illiteracy	9	1.8
Archiving	7	1.4
Saving money (reducing communication and transport costs)	6	1.2
Providing possibilities of using state-of-the-art software	6	1.2
Noted cases of under-utilization	5	1.0
Experiment to be encouraged	4	0.8
Danger for African cultures	1	0.2
Total	503	100.0

Source: Thioune and Sène, 'Inquiries and questionnaires, ICTs and Community Development Study, Senegal, November 2000' (2001).

Chapter 4

Use of ICTs: Impacts on African communities

The central hypothesis of the Acacia program is based on the perspective that new ICTs can transform communities. The objective of this section is to highlight the effects that the use of ICTs have had on the communities targeted by the projects supported by Acacia. Although it is premature at this stage of the research to conclude that ICTs have contributed significantly to the development process in Africa, some of the findings attest to emerging changes that can be attributed to ICTs and their use. These observations herald the important role that ICTs might play in community development in Africa if significant constraints were lifted.

This chapter describes the effects or changes experienced by ICT users in communities in Kenya, Senegal, Uganda, and around the Msunduzi River in South Africa. These communities have reached different levels in their use and appropriation of ICTs. For example, in Uganda and Kenya, the communities surveyed generally do not use the new ICTs. However, in Senegal the communities do use them and they have started to apply them to their various activities (mainly at the individual level). In South Africa, the community around the Msunduzi River has used ICTs in natural resource management.

The projects initiated in the first phase of the Acacia program were mainly meant for demonstration and experimentation and, on average, had a 2-year duration. The research revealed – and confirmed by users themselves – that ICTs had some effects on individual users and community organizations. We can therefore infer that the transforming effects of ICTs are visible right from the early stage of their use.

Development is a dynamic and iterative process that unfolds over time. Processes are very important to the understanding of observed changes. This section analyses the process of ICT introduction against the backdrop of global technological innovation. Accordingly, it is important to highlight the changes in community perceptions and behaviours that occur as ICTs are introduced and appropriated. These are separate from the real changes or effects that resulted from the introduction and use of ICTs in individual and community activities.

Changes in perceptions and behaviours

In Uganda and Kenya where the new ICTs had not yet been introduced by the projects, most of the rural communities believe that computers are not made for them. It was mainly the community leaders and project heads who had used or heard about ICTs who believed that they could be useful tools for development.

In Senegal, where the new ICTs have been introduced in the communities surveyed (even in non-electrified areas), it was evident that this was the first access and physical contact that the communities had had with the new ICTs. Most of the respondents believed that the access to ICTs in their communities constituted a great change in both their environment and behaviours. Users who had been in contact with ICTs felt that their standing had increased, especially among those who know how to use and manipulate these tools.

The use of ICTs increases the visibility of the villages, which in turn stimulates its economic potential. Community leaders increasingly participate in forums and seminars where they can make contacts, learn from the experiences of others, and generally increase their knowledge and share it with their constituents. Examples of these interactions include participation in the "Africa Connects Conference: Education in the Internet Age" project and participation in methodological workshops and seminars organized by Acacia and ELSA.

Interviews with some community groups highlighted how perceptions and behaviours toward ICTs have changed over time as these groups increased their contact with these tools. The following changes were noted:

•   At first, ICTs represent a myth for those who have not been trained in or in contact with these technologies (especially with regard to computers and the Internet) – they are considered to be a luxury reserved for the "intellectuals."

- After the community groups have been in contact with these technologies, they express curiosity and willingness to discover more about them – demystification is underway.
- The next stage occurs when there is a show of interest, especially by use rs who have discovered the potential of these technologies and who have developed new needs in relation to them (e.g., needs for training and equipment and for various types of information).

Communities were dynamic in their behaviour toward ICTs. First, they showed curiosity, then a desire to learn more, and finally a process to adopt ICTs is triggered, which suggests a form of social ownership. This appropriation process is more rapid when people are trained to use these tools. User behaviour with regard to ICTs also changes over time. After users are trained, they develop technical and organizational skills, which they use not only for their activities but also for the organizations and institutions to which they belong. In addition, trained users were observed to use ICTs more and more regularly.

However, the great majority of the population, who are potential users of ICTs, do not yet see a link, or an even remote relationship, between the use of ICTs and the improvement of their economic and social conditions. A comment made by a community leader in Maka Coulibantang, in Senegal, is quite revealing:

> We want to know how the computer and Internet can improve our living conditions. We know that with a well we have access to water, which we use for our market gardening so we can make more money to buy food and also improve our food diet. But as far as ICTs are concerned, you need to show us how this is possible.

This same perception is noted in Uganda, where many potential users do not always see the usefulness of ICTs (Table 12) and others feel that they are not yet ready to use them:

> For the small business that I'm running, ICTs do not mean anything…these sophisticated machines are not made for people like us. How can those

39

machines be of any help? They are maybe useful to educated people who have big businesses to run (A Woman in Uganda, November 2000).

ICTs remain a mystery for the majority of the people...they do not understand things like computers, Internet, email, and other modern means of communication. This might be explained by the fact that they are ignorant or that these technologies are beyond their reach; however, it could also be explained by the fact that they attach little importance to information compared with other more urgent problems such as poverty, healthcare, children's education, and marketing of agricultural products (Community Leader, Kabale District, Uganda, November 2000).

Some community leaders who have been made aware of the potential role of ICTs for development foresee the positive transformative effects of their use:

Our farmers are facing numerous agricultural problems. Information is the key to solving part of these problems, and hence, to development. An ICT project would be useful if it meets farmers' expectations and information needs. Information is an essential resource for the modernization of agriculture (Director of Production and Marketing, Kabale Local Committee, Uganda).

Changes observed by ICT users in their activities

Put at the disposal of communities, ICTs can become important tools that enable them to enhance both community and individual activities. In the projects discussed here, due to many factors, many of those surveyed did not notice any major changes resulting from the use of ICTs. However, some people noted some changes following the introduction of ICTs in their environment. In Uganda, in communities where the new ICTs have not yet been used, only 45 people observed changes, and these were mainly the result of the use of the telephone. Under the CEEWA project, which aimed to build the capacities of women entrepreneurs through ICTs and training (mainly managerial skills), some women in Buwama, Nabweru, and Kampala noted changes in their economic activities (e.g., small businesses, arts and crafts, pottery, sewing, and hairdressing).

In Senegal, where the new ICTs were actually introduced and used in the communities surveyed, 153 people (about 50% of users surveyed) observed changes that could be traced to ICTs. The range of projects in Senegal was more variable than in the other countries, and only 11% of the 312 users noted improvements in their trade activities, 3.5% in health activities, and 6.7% in agricultural activities.

The major changes that were reported by the studies conducted in Senegal, Uganda, and South Africa, can be summed up in the following areas: capacity building, better sanitary conditions, better educational conditions, higher income, employment generation, higher production, greater involvement in community matters, greater involvement of women and youth in productive activities, improvement of contacts with family members, access to information, and introduction of new values. Some of these changes are discussed in more detail.

Individual capacity building

This oft-cited change in the study is derived from computer and other training programs conducted as part of the Acacia projects. Part of the change can also be attributed to increased use of ICTs. Capacity building in Uganda was linked mainly to the training program set up by CEEWA. In this project, women were able to start up economic activities after they received training. In fact, 69 out of the 90 women surveyed were trained in the management of small- and medium-sized enterprises: 53.6% of them acquired the capacity to calculate cost and benefits; 24.6% the capacity to monitor their activities; 10.1% developed skills in customer service; 4.3% learned to keep statistics; and 11.6% became more experienced in their work.

In addition, 78% of the women who were trained also trained their children, partners, neighbours, or relatives and acquaintances. Capacity building in Uganda was more the result of training in the management of a micro-enterprise rather than in the use of new ICTs. Although the observed changes do not seem to have direct links with ICTs, what is important is not really the ICTs (the technologies) but rather the content they convey. The capacities developed by these women might be used to create appropriate content for the ICT tools. With their acquired skills, ICTs provide women entrepreneur with tools that enable them to achieve higher income and to increase the outlets for their products (Table 13).

In Senegal, the statistics obtained from quantitative investigations (Table 14) (Thioune and Sène 2001) revealed that individual capacity building is mainly linked to the capacity to use computers for word processing and data applications (60.2% of the users). Capacities were also developed in other sectors although their current use is still marginal (e.g., web site design, programming, and computer maintenance). Organizational capacities were also developed as a result of the use of ICTs and the training received (e.g., in management, data processing, and maintenance) both at work and in other areas.

Education and educational activities

In Uganda, only 5.1% of respondents declared that they felt the effect of ICTs in their educational activities. The study did not specify how these conditions improved. In Senegal, 27.8% of respondents said they had acquired better knowledge, and 6.5% declared that they understood their lessons better because they were better presented and the teachers had improved the course contents. ICTs have also contributed to improving and increasing communication flows between the pupils and the teaching staff according to 13% of the respondents. School community members also said that they had easier access to current literature and data (6.5%).

In addition to quantitative data, individual and group interviews were conducted in youth cyber spaces in Senegal. The teaching staff reported better school performance by pupils who frequently go to youth cyber spaces and significantly greater participation in classes. Pupils with access to information other than that provided by the teacher increasingly participate in classes and obtain higher marks. Some of the teaching staff confessed that the fact that some pupils frequently go to youth cyber spaces forces them, in turn, to further improve the content of their classes to keep pace with the pupils. The pupils reported that they seek more information to better prepare for the classes given by their teachers and also to avoid being "ridiculed" for not knowing about different subjects.

Family relations

Both in Uganda and Senegal, the potential to use ICTs for communication seems to be largely exploited (telephone in Senegal and Uganda, and mainly email in Senegal). Users now feel closer to their families and friends who reside in places scattered around the world (whether within the country or abroad) and also save money by avoiding travel. It is mainly traditional ICTs, such as the telephone that are used most often.

Trade activities and the workplace

For these sectors, time-saving seems to be the most important result achieved. These savings are mentioned by entrepreneurs who maintain business relations with partners scattered both inside and especially outside Africa. These people use the telephone and email most often and said that they now feel closer to their partners and have been able to increase the outlets for their goods and services. The following examples, which are extracted from interviews with entrepreneurs and ICT users, illustrate how ICTs have been used.

Through the TPS units in Senegal, a few entrepreneurs have been able to enter into partnership with foreign traders through the Internet to expand their economic activities. For example, the leader of a Podor-based enterprise known as GIE Sahel Agro-Enterprise established a partnership through the Internet. He received samples of pesticides and introduced them to farmers for testing. He now fills regular orders from the farmers at competitive prices, and reported that this activity had become thriving.

In another example, a baker, who happened to share the same building with a TPS unit in Joal-Fadiouth, frequently visited the centre to ask the managers for information. He finally acquired a computer and has now computerized his business management system, although he only has an intermediate-level education (6 years of study in the Senegalese educational system).

Through the national TPS network, a market for local agricultural products has been organized to link surplus and deficit areas. Onion producers in Podor (Saint-Louis region) were able to use the TPS infrastructure to dispose of their surplus production by selling it to traders based in the Thiès region who had expressed their need through the TPS web site.

Nevertheless, some users are growing impatient to see results from the use of the Internet and are embittered: the leader of an organization based in Thiès (Senegal) declared:

I subscribed to the unit and always pay money to connect to the Internet to find partners who potentially can help me take out a patent for my inventions. I was made to believe that I could easily find partners on the Internet with whom to do business. Yet, I am more and more tempted not to spend my money anymore by connecting to the Internet knowing that so far I've not had any results.

This raises the crucial problem about the perception that the people and potential users have of the Internet. They begin to believe that this tool can solve all problems. A second equally important problem is how the information that can be found might be relevant to the needs of the users.

Observed effects of ICTs in communities

Although the most obvious changes seem to directly affect individuals at the community level, interviews with some community groups revealed some significant effects (Tables 14 and 15) (Thioune and Sène 2001).

Development of organizational and consultative capacities

Some managers of community telecentres cited the development of organizational and consultative capacities as a direct result of ICT use. Although some organizational skills were developed with the use of ICT and telecentre services, organizational skills needed by rural communities to face the challenges and requirements of the world market are still lacking. They must learn to obtain value for money, organize production in great quantities and quality, and create networks to obtain economies of scale and synergistic effects.

Direct job creation

One of the important effects resulting from the introduction of ICTs in poor or marginalized areas is employment generation. Generally, members of the community hosting the projects hold these jobs. For example, in Senegal, sixteen managers of CRCs (including ten women), twelve managers of TPS units, and four managers of CICs have been recruited in the sites hosting the projects. This has contributed to an increase in community interest in the new ICTs because people see that ICTs can create jobs in communities where unemployment is widespread. In addition to the jobs generated directly, income is distributed to other groups (e.g., maintenance agents, trainers, SONATEL, and SENELEC). In Senegal, because of the increase in the number of individuals who have acquired skills in the ICT sector, the employment-generation effect in the rural areas will probably be reinforced.

Capacity building in management

There is an apparent reinforcement of management capacities in communities, notably in general accounting, planning, communication, and organization. For example, the Baraka centre in Senegal became, thanks to counselling by the managers, the management hub for community activities. This was also the case in Joal, where community accounting was completely automated. The local councillors noted that the direct effect of this innovation was improved transparency in the management of local affairs. With their training, managers are positioning themselves on the national and even international employment scene (three of the ENDA CRC managers and two former heads of TPS units are in Europe or USA, where they were reportedly earning much more money). However, while this may be viewed as a success at the individual level, it is a deplorable situation for the community because one of the effects expected from ICTs and related projects was the stabilization of rural-urban migration by creating employment in rural areas.

Structuring effects of ICTs for community organizations

In Senegal, the community organizations involved in the projects seem to have been transformed by the use of ICTs. This is most evident in their operations: keying in meeting reports, better organization of documents, and higher visibility for documents because they are better presented. In South Africa, the communities participating in the Msunduzi project were linked through a web site that facilitated communication. Through this site, organizations had greater visibility and were able to secure more easily financial and training support from their partners. However, the effectiveness of this web site as a means of communication and training for the local populace and their environment, as a form of knowledge transfer, was not apparent.

Process of social rehabilitation and inclusion

Some of the people surveyed in the underprivileged districts of Dakar, Senegal feel that their social standing has increased and that their districts and marginalized groups (women, youth, and the illiterate) have been socially rehabilitated. The residents of shantytowns like Colobane, Gouye Mouride, and Baraka, have gained confidence, although the majority are illiterate. In addition, the richer neighbouring districts have been showing a growing interest in these districts. For example, the Baraka district was once considered the refuge of dropouts, but today it welcomes the well-to-do residents of neighbouring districts who come there to navigate on the Web. The residents of these districts now talk with a lot of pride about themselves and their districts, which have now become safer places. This is an important result. Even if most of the population do not use ICT services, the simple fact that the new tools exist restores their confidence and helps them to envisage a future with more hope and to expend more energy to improve their living conditions: "The CRC saved us ... we are now socializing ... before, we were real aggressors" (a resident of Cité du Rail, Dakar).

Raising awareness of social problems

In Senegal, young people and women who frequently go to youth cyber spaces are reported to have heightened awareness of AIDs and sexually transmitted diseases (STD). GEEP organizes a contest related to sex education every year. In their preparations, the contestants look for information on the Internet. This broadens their knowledge of both ICTs and health issues. This awareness is an important result because it shows how new ICTs can play a role in a very sensitive area. Young people can look for information directly without any intermediary. In that way, they avoid the social and cultural taboos surrounding matters related to sex and to sexually transmitted diseases such as AIDS. Another phenomenon was observed when young people and teachers used the youth cyber spaces. As a result of their involvement, some of the pupils initiated teachers and adults in the use of ICTs. In South Africa, community organizations in the area of the Msunduzi River exhibited better understanding and heightened awareness of environmental and natural resource problems.

Gradual integration of ICTs into community life

ICTs exert some fascination, which is characterized by a strong demand for computer training among young people. Young people do adopt new ICTs more quickly. The fact that there was a response to this demand for training and that ICT equipment was available contributed to the building of technical and institutional capacities in the communities. Young people were trained in data processing and various services (e.g., telephones, office equipment, and information) were provided to entrepreneurs, traders, and individuals.

In contrast to South Africa, where the local economy did not seem to have been affected by the Msunduzi project, ENDA's resource centres had a positive effect on local economic activities in Senegal. In fact, the centres changed the structure of the communities by attracting into their surrounding environment restaurants, small businesses, and arts and crafts vendors. The communities that hosted these centres have developed improved capacities to organize and have gradually reinforced community solidarity. Also in Senegal, secondary effects on development and partnership have been observed. For example, the Baraka district is now receiving more aid from NGOs and other donors and greater attention from the public authorities. Some of the schools that hosted FLE clubs were equipped with computers donated by UNFPA, The 2/3 Canada Club (a Canadian NGO), and Schools Online (an American NGO), as part of an effort to extend research in this area.

The human resources within these districts have become increasingly developed. Participation in community activities (e.g., information and exposure to ICTs, financial and material participation, and equipment management and upkeep) is correlated to project activities in general in Uganda, Senegal, and South Africa.

Emergence of a virtual community

The study identified correspondence between members of the same family and between friends as an important motive for using ICTs. The main benefits mentioned by respondents was *bringing family members and friends closer together* by facilitating direct and almost instantaneous interaction between people located in very distant places. These remote contacts with family members also contribute to maintaining family ties regardless of the distance. Migration is a very important phenomenon in Africa where the working

47

population, severely affected by structural unemployment, is increasingly tempted to migrate to Europe and North America. The following statement confirms that ICTs can play a role in the economic and social development of the community:

> A tangible and palpable effect is how the community of Joal benefited this year when a young member of the community, who was residing in Europe, found on the Internet a description of the needs and activities of the residents of his rural district. He reacted by sending computer equipment and medicines. It is also interesting that Joal had an Internet connection before one of its European "twin sisters." This fact encouraged this city in the North to create its own web site. It has now clearly overtaken us; just because it had greater means and also because its authorities grasped the stakes of the new economy. (Statement made by Mamadou Sarr, a local official and member of the Joal TPS Management Committee, at the Feedback Workshop on ICTs and Community Development, Senegal, July 2001)

However, if ICTs are not regulated to a certain extent, they can worsen imbalances or inequalities. This is particularly true with regard to individual or group access to resources that are scarce, and in the case of new ICT tools, which can be considered by some to confer "prestige" on its users.

Developing resource control strategies

In the communities that hosted the projects, there were reports of groups of individuals (e.g., management committee or project staff) usurping resources to the exclusion of other individuals or groups This is one reason why in Maka Coulibantang in Senegal, the establishment of a CIC could not restore dialogue and understanding between the rival villages of Maka and Coulibantang, which nonetheless are in charge of this project from an institutional and managerial point of view. The centre was underutilized by residents of Maka, which hosts the CIC and is also the administrative centre for the Maka Coulibantang rural community. The tendency to control resources is also reflected in the management of some youth cyber spaces in which the teaching staff was reportedly inclined to "monopolize" equipment at the expense of the pupils.

Unequal access of women to ICTs

These studies revealed that there was a clear difference between men and women in terms of access to the services and content of ICTs. Within the communities, more men use ICTs than women due to many factors (e.g., level of education and income). But women who do use ICTs look for more information than men, who instead use ICTs mainly as a means of communication. This is indicative of the quality or level of education of the women who have access to ICTs. In Senegal, the average level of education of women ICT users is the secondary education level. In youth cyber spaces in Senegal, among students, gender parity and equality appeared to have been respected both in terms of committee membership and access to services. A synergy was also created between the secondary schools hosting the youth cyberspaces and other institutions that requested use of the services. This resulted in the creation of successful partnerships in some cases.

Inappropriate uses of ICTs

With the diversity and multiplicity of information sources and types, there is a risk that ICTs might be diverted toward inappropriate uses. In fact, some of the respondents in the youth cyber spaces declared that they visited pornographic web sites instead of educational ones, which disturbed the teachers.

Conclusion

It is generally admitted that ICTs have the potential to help poor communities in sub-Saharan Africa to find new ways of accelerating their development process. The implicit hypothesis is that because development is neither a linear nor unitary process, the transforming nature of ICTs can be used to catalyze rapid and sustainable economic and social development. ICT-enabled developed countries have been able to take maximum advantage of the opportunities that these tools can offer. Therefore, poor countries and communities should be able to take advantage of these new tools to improve their capacities to create wealth and reach an improved level of development.

The study demonstrates that ICTs can meet the hopes expected of their use. ICTs are used today to varying degrees in different sectors of economic and social life. They are used to reinforce the regularity of communication and exchange of information between scattered family members; to design registration forms; to improve agricultural production and productivity; to gain access to markets; to enhance school performance; to modernize the management of enterprises in the informal sector; to combat insecurity; and to save time and money.

The impact of ICTs could be increased by ensuring that content is adapted to the conditions of the targeted populations and by finding ways to increase access for rural populations. Furthermore, economic development should be based on sectors that have a comparative advantage. In this perspective, if the conditions of access to ICT are fulfilled, the rural world (made up of about 70% of the working population) could be an economic lever in the context of globalization, in which information is an important and relatively cheap production factor.

The experiment conducted under VCMR in Senegal demonstrated the roles that ICTs can play in a rural environment among users with limited education. In this project, ICTs played a role in local governance and in rural resource management. Community leaders received tools that improved their decision-making and increased transparency in the management of their rural districts. They were also able to combine traditional and new technologies to improve the level of acceptance of new ICTs.

It is difficult at our present state of knowledge and experience in the use of ICTs to affirm with certainty that they have actually contributed to development in a quantitative and sustainable way. Although development is a dynamic process, the results of the research conducted under the Acacia program confirmed that the process of social appropriation of ICTs is well under way in some communities. Moreover, ICTs are being used (certainly still on a limited scale) to solve communication problems, to access relevant information, and to better organize economic and community activities. However, the process of appropriating and using ICTs on a large scale in poor communities is still hindered by many institutional, technical, economic, and socio-cultural constraints.

Table 12: Opinion of respondents on the usefulness of ICT content in Uganda

Usefulness Rating	Number	Percentage
Very useful	17	43.6
Fairly useful	3	7.7
Not useful	2	5.1
Not sure/no opinion	17	43.6
Total	39	100.0

Source: Etta et al. (2001).

Table 13: Changes occurring in communities that were attributed to ICTs (Uganda)

Observed changes	Nature of change	Number	%
1. Capacity building	Use of computer	5	6.4
	Employment opportunity	1	1.3
	Improved communication	2	2.6
	Modernization	2	2.6
	Achieving individual potential	2	2.6
	Not specified	2	2.6
2. Health and sanitation	Health information available	3	3.8
	Not specified	2	2.6
3. Improvement of teaching conditions	Generation of little money	1	1.3
	Capacity building	4	5.1
4. Increased income	Income generation	2	3.6
5. Job creation	Job	13	16.7
	Increased income	1	1.3
	Not specified	1	1.3
6. Improvements in agric. production	Improvement of farming methods and techniques	2	2.6
7. Greater involvement in community matters	Security	1	1.3

Table 13: Continued

Observed changes	Nature of change	Number	%
8. Improvement of conditions of women and youth	Improvement of status	4	5.1
	Acquisition of new skills by the young (e.g., email and facsimile)	1	1.3
9. Better use of information	Improvements in communications	7	9.0
	Easy contact with business traders	1	1.3
10. Improvements in contacts and communication with relatives and friends residing outside the	Increased communication and reduced costs village/city	17	20.5
11. Loss of traditional values		0	0.0
12. Introduction of new values	Modernization	2	2.6
	Internet services	1	1.3
Total		77	100

Source: Etta et al. (2001).

Table 14: Changes observed by individual users in Senegal (2000)

Area of change	Types of change	Number	%
Acquired capacities	Word processing	141	44.2
	Navigation on the Internet	65	20.4
	Expertise in data processing	51	16
	Better work quality	13	4.1
	Easy external contact	10	3.1
	Writing computer programs	9	2.8
	Ability to process data more efficiently	8	2.5
	Faster work pace	7	2.2
	Courses prepared more efficiently	4	1.3
	Better work coordination	3	0.9
	Full vision of opportunities	3	0.9
	Computer maintenance	2	0.6
	Games	2	0.6
	Web site design	1	0.3
Total		319	100
Workplace	Time saving	73	28.1
	Higher work output	42	16.1
	Better work organization	38	18.1
	Better quality of work	37	14.2
	Easier access to information	27	10.4
	Keeping in touch with partners	21	8.1
	Easy document processing	9	3.5
	Archiving	8	3.1
	Save money	7	2.7
Total		262	100

Table 14: Continued

Area of change	Types of change	Number	%
Family relations	Easy contact	55	26.3
	Steadier relations	46	22
	Improvements in relations	27	12.9
	Faster contacts	22	10.5
	Time saving	22	10.5
	Keep in touch with relatives/friends	19	9.1
	Making savings	13	6.2
	Secure email	3	1.4
	More affection	1	0.5
Total		208	100
Trade activities	Easy contact with partners	15	37.5
	Faster work performance	6	15
	Direct contact	5	12.5
	Time saving	5	12.5
	Better outlets	4	10
	Profitability	3	7,5
	Access to more information	2	5
Total		40	100
Teaching activities	Increased knowledge	30	27.8
	Easy documentation	14	13
	Research made easier	13	12
	More exchange with colleagues/pupils	10	9.3
	Easier access to information	9	8.3
	Work made easier	9	8.3
	Data update	7	6.5
	Better understanding of courses	7	6.5

Table 14: Continued

Area of changes	Types of changes	Number	%
	Time saving	3	2.8
	Archiving	2	1.9
	Improved course contents	2	1.9
	Possibility of reading newspapers	1	0.9
	Pupils get higher marks	1	0.9
Total		108	100
Health sector	Better awareness	6	54.5
	Better knowledge	3	27.3
	Better working conditions	2	18.2
Total		11	100
Agricultural sector	Higher productivity	10	33.3
	Contact made easier	6	20
	Diversified partnership	4	13.3
	Data search	3	10
	Better knowledge in this area	3	10
	Work faster	3	10
	Easier access to financing	1	3.3
Total		30	100

Source: Thioune and Sène (2001).

Table 15: Changes observed in organizations in Senegal

Observed changes	Staff	Percentage
Easier contact with partners	28	16.1
Faster work performance	21	12.1
Better organization	20	11.5
Ability to manipulate computers	16	9.2
Higher performance	15	8.6
Increased membership	13	7.5
Improved documents	10	5.7
Exchange between partners	10	5.7
Better knowledge	9	5.2
Archiving	7	4.0
Improved income	5	2.9
Improved activities	5	2.9
More motivation	5	2.9
Capacity building	4	2.3
More reliable management	3	1.7
Higher credibility for organization	2	1.1
Job creation	1	0.6
Total	174	100.0

Source: Thioune and Sène (2001).

Chapter 5

Introduction and appropriation of ICTs: Challenges and prospects

It is generally believed that the new ICTs can offer real opportunities to improve the quality of community life. It is also important to deepen our level of reflection on community dynamics and on the constraints encountered when introducing and using ICTs for development.

This chapter seeks to identify the main challenges and problems that were encountered in the process of using ICTs for development in the research conducted under the Acacia program between 1997 and 2000. Naturally, the geographic, socio-cultural, economic, and political contexts of the countries and communities are different. The communities surveyed have, to varying degrees, familiarized themselves with the use of ICTs; however, a number of common problems were identified through the research. And in all projects, ICTs were introduced not only from the perspective of connectivity; they were meant to be integrated into development issues within communities in which the tools were to support.

Community involvement

Community development is a participatory process that must be appropriated by all components of a given community. A key observation in the projects studied was the level of participation of the populations in the process of introducing ICTs. Given the transforming nature of ICTs, it is essential to ensure community participation in all the stages of intorducing ICTs. Appropriation helps guarantee the sustainability of any development action, and more specifically innovative actions. The results of this study demonstrate that roles and responsibilities of community members evolve over time as a function of project stages and phases.

The participatory process

Launching the project in the community

Given that the great majority of the population have limited knowledge of ICTs, community involvement at the onset of the project is very often limited to a small number of dynamic, avant-garde community leaders who are project initiators. In this case, the community leader is either an elected person or simply a community leader who is credited with a degree of open-mindedness and who participates actively in community activities. Generally, these leaders are found in groups or individuals who have been directly or indirectly in contact with ICTs or who simply have innovative attitudes and who are above all "risk-takers." These leaders are able to develop strategies for working and interacting with different communities (especially rural ones). Because they are often knowledgeable in popular dynamics, and they serve as points of access to the communities, these leaders provide a valuable contribution by developing strategies designed to identify and involve dynamic groups who are likely to use ICTs in the early stages of the project.

In **Kenya,** a group of women were trained before the governance project was launched. This training enabled them to understand the potential advantages of the project and to share their views with other community members. These women were also able to express their own information and communication needs and were therefore more likely to take advantage of ICTs and seek ways to sustain their introduction in the community.

In **South Africa,** a similar approach was used. Many training modules were offered in the Msunduzi project to organizational representatives. This established the basis for their participation in project implementation and helped them to put in place a network to exchange information between various components of the project.

In **Senegal,** a participatory approach was also used in the very early stages of the process of ICT introduction. In a pro-active approach, research institutions (e.g., WARF, GEEP, and ENDA) with some experience in working with grassroots communities were identified to initiate development actions. A series of training programs was offered in how to use office equipment, standard word processing applications, Internet and email, and financial management.

The first group of people trained and involved in project management should transfer what they have learned to a larger group of people by setting up local training activities. This knowledge transfer was not always realized because of constraints faced by the Acacia project in Senegal and the Msunduzi project in South Africa. The main constraints included equipment not being available, poor project management, and poorly trained managers. In the community projects in Uganda and Kenya that were reviewed, this expansion of training could not be carried out because the project equipment had not yet been installed.

Uptake by the community

In the next stage, the communities developed their own strategies designed to use and appropriate ICTs. This was done first within the project and later within the community as a whole. For example, the youth cyber space project initiated by GEEP in Senegal used ICTs to improve communication between different FLE clubs. The ICTs hasten the process of information exchange both between these clubs and between the clubs and project administrators. The TPS units also used ICTs to transmit accounting and financial data to their parent company based in Dakar. This information was used regularly as control data to manage the project and its various subunits.

Through awareness and training strategies, the people started gradually to show a growing interest in ICTs within their communities. They participated actively in this process (either in-kind or financially) and started to use ICT services across board by both individuals and public or private organizations. In most cases, the users take advantage of the equipment and systems, but do not participate in either their purchase or operation. In addition to the participatory process, mechanisms and structures were put in place to support participation. In fact, consultative frameworks were generally set up at the instigation of the community leaders who were involved in initiating the projects.

Consultative framework

Community contributions (e.g., material contributions, adequate premises, and access to a telephone line and electricity) and formal project management structures were important parts of the participatory approach. A second important component was the establishment of management

61

committees that represented the whole community. Community leaders and management committee members used local channels of traditional communication and local authorities (e.g., local and traditional bodies, traditional chiefs, and local representatives of the administration) to reach all members of the community and also to integrate the project into the social fabric of the community.

In the process of project implementation, the management committees experienced some problems such as irremovable members, members' age, gender disparity in membership, limited logistic and financial means, and divergent needs. Studies have demonstrated that young people are the main users of ICTs and that women represent a large part of the working population, notably in the rural areas. Therefore, it is important to reflect these groups in the membership of the management committees.

Participation is essential for any action to influence individuals or their community. One way to measure this participation is to gauge the level and intensity of the people's reactions to a given action. It is also necessary to clearly differentiate the type and mode of participation as well as the participants during the different stages of project implementation. During the project-launching phase, it is important to clearly target participants at the risk of seeing the projects rejected by the communities. It is important to identify people with innovative attitudes to serve as points of entry into the community. In addition, the research in Uganda and Senegal revealed that it is very useful to use local and traditional communication channels to encourage large-scale appropriation and integration of ICTs into the communities.

Community response

The analyses of the research showed that community response to ICTs is very dynamic. The response varies over time according to the amount of information delivered to the community and the level of usefulness that communities expect from the ICTs. Although this response can be measured by the level of use, the research revealed that many other factors lead to people having a fairly passive response to ICTs (e.g., level of education, information, involvement, and training in ICTs).

Training appears to be an important element in the process of appropriation of ICTs. For example, with training and a good awareness campaign in the CEEWA project, most of the beneficiaries felt they had a good understanding of the opportunities that ICTs can offer. In Senegal, the research revealed that the uneducated populations who were not trained in ICTs had passive attitudes toward these tools. Their perceptions were based on the tools themselves and not on the content they could deliver. In fact, most of the community members think that ICTs "have not been made for them because they are poor and uneducated." This perception can be explained by the fact that the level of information on ICTs is limited to the equipment alone. Not enough emphasis is placed on the "tool" – the catalyst leading to information and knowledge.

Some potential users do not use ICTs even when they are well informed of the advantages and opportunities that ICTs can offer. For example, the case study in Senegal demonstrated that the great majority of individuals, who were aware that ICTs are useful, do not use them and adopt wait-and-see attitudes. Similar observations were made by Adam and Wood (1999) in Ethiopia. Using a qualitative approach, they found that information on ICTs was not a sufficient condition for their immediate adoption. Adoption requires a long learning period and substantial investments, and often conditions are not met in projects. Therefore, in addition to sustained briefing and awareness sessions, training and technical capacity-building sessions are necessary to encourage potential users to use ICTs.

Use of ICTs

Access to information is deemed crucial to development during this era of a global economy supported by electronic communications. In the Acacia-supported projects that were studied, all social categories, all social groups, and all corporate bodies were to have access to the services provided after the equipment was made available. However, given the novelty of these tools and a combination of many factors, some groups or individuals do not have full access to ICTs. Factors such as age, education level, income, and location limit access to the new ICTs.

The research findings seem to indicate (at least with community access points) that the use of ICTs varied across age groups. Young people (age group 18–35 years) seem to be the most regular users of ICT services (Figure 2). The young were also the most educated in the areas studied (mainly rural or suburban areas), most of them run a profit-making economic activity (in the primary or informal sector), and they were generally active in community associations and organizations. These young people use, in order of importance, email, the Internet, and word processing to find penpals and financial partners, send or receive messages or mail, key in and edit document, and train in data processing. Adults (age group 36–55 years) use, in order of importance, office equipment, telephones, the Internet, and email mainly to key in and edit documents, train in word processing, and find commercial outlets, partners, and business opportunities.

Although the use of the new ICTs is very limited in Kenya and Uganda, it is important to note that in regions where they are now being used, the communities have started to apply them to solve their own problems. They are being used to access specific information, for communication, to design working documents, and for keeping the accounts of organizations and small- and medium-sized enterprises (e.g., arts and crafts traders). The web site established as part of the Msunduzi project in South Africa made it possible, through the networking of community organizations, to collect and disseminate information on the environment. This allowed the communities involved in the project to better manage their own natural resources. In Senegal, community organizations and entrepreneurs, among others, have started to use the new ICTs in their every-day activities.

Figure 2: Age distribution of users of new ICTs

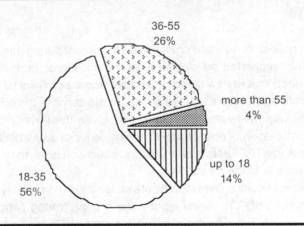

Source: 'Inquiries and questionnaires, ICTs and Community Development Study, Senegal,' November 2000 (Thioune and Sene 2001).

There is also an emerging social appropriation of new ICTs. In fact, in some communities, such as Baraka and Rail in Dakar (Senegal), ICTs are perceived as a means of social rehabilitation and inclusion. In these communities, having an email address or using word processing to prepare accounting documents (e.g., invoices, receipts, budget, and balance sheets) is considered a sign of modernity by the arts and crafts workers. Having a telephone line enhances the standing of domestic servants from these neighbourhoods once considered to be inhabited only by dropouts.

The majority of people or groups who frequently go to community access points and request the services of ICTs, use them more or less regularly after their first contact with these tools (Figure 3) (Thioune and Sene 2001). They are generally willing to go (from the village to the city) to where they can use the services. This shows that people will not be attracted by ICTs (or any other technology) unless they find them to be useful. After they discover them through awareness campaigns and actually use them, they will be much more likely to integrate their use into their everyday life.

Although some individuals or communities have started using ICTs, the great majority of the people in these communities do not use them. Even among those who use ICTs, some have started to question their relevance (particularly access to the Internet). For example, some entrepreneurs in the region of Thiès (Senegal) immediately joined the registered trade system when the TPS unit was opened. This gave them access to trade information and allowed them to pursue business opportunities. They were very enthusiastic at the beginning, and most used the TPS system to offer their goods and services and to seek business opportunities. However, most of these first subscribers now go to these units much less frequently because the trade information they want is rarely available. And the search for information is not free. Therefore, the demand for these services within the TPS units has fallen.

Furthermore, most entrepreneurs who were potential users of this type of service adopted a wait-and-see attitude. They wanted to see concrete evidence that other entrepreneurs had been able to benefit from business opportunities presented by the Internet. This shows the importance of sensitization and the demonstration of the opportunities that ICTs can offer. It also points to the need to establish a network between different communities to share their experiences with a view to learning from each other and to disseminating the lessons arising from community use of ICTs. Notable efforts were made to establish such networks under the Acacia-supported projects in Senegal, but the results seemed not to match expectations. This suggests there is a need to continue to seek appropriate sensitization and demonstration strategies, methods, and materials to reach the majority of potential users better.

A distinction should also be made between the direct users of the equipment and applications and the users of the information. In fact, experience has shown that although the equipment is used most often, there is still no systematic use of the information drawn from the various existing materials. Such is the case, for example, in the VCMR project in Senegal. The project developed, in collaboration with the Cheikh Anta Diop University of Dakar, and on the basis of the needs identified by the people, resources on health, natural resource management (NRM), and management of community development projects. These resources, though corresponding to the community needs expressed at participatory diagnosis sessions, were not used. The people do, however, request registration forms and word processing services. Therefore, there is a need to determine the order of priorities as well as the information needs, which, of course, keep changing.

Figure 3: Frequency of use of ICTs

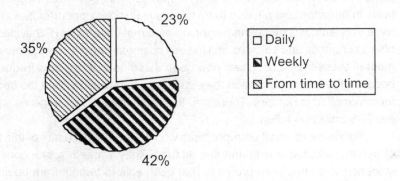

Source: 'Inquiries and questionnaires, ICTs and Community Development Study, Senegal,' November 2000 (Thioune and Sène 2001).

The research also revealed that ICTs are regularly and mainly used for social reasons, and especially to respond to community needs. In fact, ICTs are generally used to contact family members residing in different parts of the world (thus creating a virtual community). The ICTs are mostly used as communication tools; little use is made of their informative potential. Although there were a few reported cases of the use of ICTs to seek information that would serve as inputs or production factors, the potential of ICTs as decision-making instruments is not yet systematically exploited. Nonetheless, ICTs and the information they convey can have a transforming effect when they are used to accommodate user needs. Therefore, they can contribute significantly to the transformation of working methods and processes.

Experience with the TPS units in Senegal revealed that although sources of information are available, entrepreneurs rarely used them. The trade information that was available was generally suited to a structured and well-organized market with sufficient infrastructure. This was not the case in the rural economies in the communities surveyed. These are rather informal economies in "pre-market" situations. Therefore, innovative ways must be found to rapidly integrate these users into this more formal and more structured market, which is both internal and external to the country.

The use of ICTs is currently limited communication, which is of course important because it corresponds to a need expressed by the people. However, there is little use of their informative potential. The challenge is therefore to find appropriate sensitization and demonstration strategies, methods, and materials that will allow the majority of potential users to become aware of the existing relevant information that can be conveyed by ICTs.

What role for women?

It is generally believed that access to information is correlated with access to power, be it economic or political power. The desire for equity and social justice demands that women become active participants and take advantage of the benefits that ICTs can offer. Technological changes can be used to promote improvements in their economic and social conditions, bearing in mind that they represent generally more than half of the population. This issue of access by women is all the more important and urgent because

ICTs are expected to play an expanding role in economic and social development. However, research shows that there is a great disparity between men and women in terms of access to ICTs and information.

Although it is proven empirically that women use ICT services in the urban, suburban, and rural areas, this use remains marginal compared with men. Overall, in Kenya, Uganda, and Senegal, women seem to be marginalized in the use of ICTs. There seems to be a tendency for traditional access and control mechanisms to apply to the use of ICTs. Study findings in Uganda and Kenya showed that where traditional technologies are mostly used (telephone, for example), women use ICTs less than men. In Senegal, where the new ICTs were actually used, the same tendencies to marginalize women were revealed in the use of ICTs.

Figure 4: Gender distribution of users of new ICTs

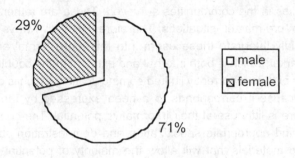

Source: Thioune and Sène, 'Inquiries and questionnaires, ICTs and Community Development Study, Senegal, November 2000' (2001).

According to Rathgeber (2000: 27), "feminist philosophers interested of science have observed that female cognitive structures differ from those of men. This has implications for women's attitudes and approaches to the use of ICTs." This differentiation was demonstrated in Malaysia where an inquiry into the behaviour of girls and boys in schools revealed that there is a significant difference between them in relation to the use of ICTs and to the attitudes adopted toward ICTs. According to Nor Azen et al. (2000), because boys receive more training and have more regular access to computers, they use ICTs more than girls. Unlike girls, the boys also declared that they have greater technical capacities (programming and maintenance).

A study conducted in Australia (Fluck 1995) revealed that girls use computers relatively more often than boys at school, but that boys use them twice as often outside school. Another study, conducted in Great Britain (Cole et al. 1994), found that when they are put in similar access conditions with boys, girls use computers as much as do boys, but specifically in relation to their lessons. ELSA–Acacia observed a similar tendency in its study on schools network in Senegal (Camara and Thioune 2001). The school cases seem to be different from experiences in communities. In fact, in community ICT access points (telecentres, for example), apart from considerations linked to the cognitive nature of women, exogenous factors such as income, service access costs, education level, and management mode do not seem to favour women.

In most cases, ICTs seem to be less profitable to women than men because technologies are often associated with men. Women are often more active in "non-technical" professions and generally have perceived psychological barriers toward these tools. In fact, comments from women in the case studies (in Senegal, Uganda, and Kenya) that ICTs were not made for them tend to confirm this attitude toward ICTs.

Byron and Gagliardi (1998) seem to confirm Rathgeber's (2000) assertion about a gender difference in cognitive processes. They believe indeed that "the difference in the amount of time spent using ICTs seems to have to do with attitudes as well as issues of access, boys appearing to be more process-oriented in their use, girls more goal-oriented."

The challenge faced by researchers is to find the most appropriate technological medium that can be adapted to women's conditions. However, other factors seem to contribute to the limited access of women to ICTs. Women's low level of income, limited education, and non-involvement in ICT projects seem, indeed, to constitute significant factors that limit their access to ICTs. In fact, in the sites surveyed in Senegal, women were generally not consulted during the preparatory, acquisition, installation, and ICT exploitation phases. As a result, the existing systems are generally not adapted to their needs. And yet, the involvement of women in this digital era is deemed crucial by all observers.

It appeared from the case studies that women participate actively in projects they have been involved in from the beginning. For example, in the

ENDA project headed by a woman, most of the community telecentres were either managed by a woman or by a woman and a man (mixed management). In these telecentres, women used ICTs in the same (or even higher) proportion as men. In many projects, however, gender equality is not a specific objective. As a result, when it comes to planning, it is important to think of ways to encourage women's leadership in project implementation if women are to be efficiently and successfully involved.

Obviously, projects that specifically target women attract their greater participation (e.g., CEEWA in Uganda). Available evidence suggests that women can participate fully in the development of their community through the opportunities presented by ICTs. One interesting case involved Serbatim women entrepreneurs in Dakar. Starting with a single computer, they were able to expand their computer services business by using the Internet to search for new clients. They were also able to place their children in community telecentres (job creation). Furthermore, by using their network of partners and email, these women were able to receive additional training and to participate in overseas trade fairs. In this way, they increased the visibility of their community and could tap prospective business opportunities.

Education level

Research findings revealed that regardless of the fact that most of the Acacia-supported projects are based in rural or suburban areas, users of ICTs are well educated (formal education) and most of them can read and write in English (in South Africa, Kenya, and Uganda) and French (in Senegal). A great proportion of them can also read and write at least one of their local languages. Does that mean that the uneducated are excluded from access to ICTs? It is prevalent said in the literature that limited education is one of the factors that limits access to ICTs.

Although the functional relationship between ICTs and education level was not studied, such a relationship seems to exist. It is risky to exclude the uneducated from development projects. They are greater in number in the rural areas, generally have very low literacy rates (in French and English), and represent the majority of the working population of these countries. In Senegal, for example, 70% of the working population is found in the primary sector (mainly rural). Similar proportions are observed in Uganda and Kenya. This active population should be one of the engines of growth. Therefore, the challenge is to find technological solutions that can be directly or indirectly

70

used by these people both to improve their living conditions and to participate fully in economic and social development in the context of an information economy.

The uneducated need not be totally excluded from the use of ICTs because they can get assistance from the managers of community telecentres or points of access. These people can help them with certain ICTs, such as the telephone, because the messages to be received or conveyed can be given orally and generally in the local language of the user. However, the situation is quite different when it comes to computers, the Internet, or email, which generally require the ability to read and write.

Location

The location of ICT projects seems to be an important factor in universal access. This research revealed a degree of difference between rural and urban areas. In fact, due to the quality of infrastructure and the vicinity of more formal and more structured markets, urban communities seem to benefit more from ICTs than those located in the rural areas. One can compare the sites of Maka Coulibantang in Senegal, a land-locked area without electricity, Vulindlela in South Africa, and Rubaya and Buwama in Uganda, where telephone lines are limited due to the geographic situation (mountainous and rocky area), with the school community of Lycée Blaise Diagne in Dakar, and Yeumbeul, which is located in the suburban area of Dakar. In the latter two cases, it was the high cost of service, not the absence of infrastructure, that limited the use of ICTs.

The findings of the case study on Senegal suggest that the types of applications or technologies used, the user profiles, and the number of users vary on the basis of location (urban versus rural). Tables 16 and 17 show that in Ross-Béthio, a largely rural area, telephone is used more often than in Joal, which is an urban district. However, the level of use of the new ICTs (Internet, email, and word processing) is higher in Joal than in Ross-Béthio.

The level of economic activity (and thus income availability) seems to be an important factor for differentiating between the level and type of ICT use. In Ross-Bethio, more use was made of searches for office and trade information; whereas, in Podor people used email more than any other application. Ross-Bethio is largely a farming area (irrigated farming is practised thanks to the availability of water throughout the year) with low rates of migration; whereas, Podor is rather a rural, administrative and school town, with a high migration rate.

Similar tendencies in the use of the new ICTs were observed in Uganda with respect to traditional ICTs such as the telephone. Telephones are used more often in areas closer to urban centres than in more rural areas (because of infrastructure problems and restricted availability of equipment).

Training and capacity building

Africa does not have all the technical skills required for the efficient development of ICTs, particularly because technologies are imported and are fast-changing (Lohento 2001). According to Davison et al. (2000), ICTs were developed, to a large extent, in the context and for the cultural and social standards of rich countries (i.e., Western Europe, North America, East and Southeast Asia, and Australia). In this context, an appropriation of ICTs for development implies the need to develop the indigenous technical skills needed to significantly reduce the current gap between Africa and developed countries.

Research findings show that training is essential for ICT use and appropriation. ICTs constitute a new challenge for the countries where the Acacia program is concentrated. Training and awareness campaigns appeared to be the project's first activities: training in computer use, office software applications, use of email, and Internet navigation. However, the people trained were generally those directly involved in telecentre management (operators and, to a lesser degree, management committee members on different project sites), and many community members obviously lacked appropriate training to use ICTs for their needs.

The technical skills of the managers of community access points seem to be confined to using standard applications. Generally, these managers received no technical training in maintenance of ICTs. As well, those who act as intermediaries between the demand for and supply of information also lacked the technical means and skills to collect, process, store, transform, and disseminate information through materials in different languages and channels appropriate to the end users. In the communities surveyed in Senegal and South Africa, specific training was given according to the objectives and areas of ICT application (e.g., training in web site development and maintenance, natural resource management, and financial management techniques). However, because of differences in the training standards for managers of community access points, the training could not

72

be used efficiently. There were attempts at translating training modules into local languages (Zulu in South Africa, for example), but not in a systematic way.

Another phenomenon was noted in the school environment in Senegal. Pupils played a role as trainers in some institutions. These pupils received some training through their participation in the management committees of youth cyber spaces and have provided ICT training to teachers. This is a very important outcome of the training and learning process of ICTs because younger people, who account for over half of the Senegalese population, seem to be more attracted to new ICTs than older people. This attraction of the young to the new ICTs is also observed in Uganda and Kenya.

Countries like Senegal, Kenya, and Uganda have no ICT policy, and particularly no training policy on ICTs. This limits training and hinders the process of socially appropriating ICTs. The ELSA–IDRC study (Camara and Thioune 2001) on ICTs in school communities in Senegal demonstrated that schools were rather conservative in their approach. Because the curriculum did not include any policy to integrate new ICTs, they were not used much in schools especially by school administration and teaching staff. Despite this constraint, the survey confirmed the relevance of the approach taken by the youth cyber spaces project to focus on the training of teachers and administrative officers (who seem to be most averse to change). By raising their awareness, and demonstrating to them the opportunities that the inclusion of ICTs in school curricula can offer, they were more likely to change their approach.

The analysis of training and capacity building standards revealed that the unavailability of training materials is also an important problem. The challenge is to find appropriate training formats and contents for the many and variable needs of the target communities. The most appropriate training methods and processes would also have to be determined for each community group (e.g., women, youth, and entrepreneurs).

Information delivery

The findings from these research projects revealed that mass media (television, radio, and newspapers) have played a major role in the provision of information on ICTs to the rural populations. In Senegal, radio is the main source of information on new ICTs (for 72.3% of the population) followed by television (71.6%) and newspapers (56.3%). These media are used because they are appropriate and provide easy access to information. In the context of inadequate technical infrastructure, high illiteracy rates, and relatively low income, these media can be combined with ICTs to collect, process, and disseminate information to local communities, especially in local languages.

In the current context in African countries, community access points to ICTs and telecentres seem to offer the most appropriate ways to provide broad access to ICTs. Telecentre operators can serve as important information relays to potential users by finding, processing, and storing useful information on media that can be used by local populations to help achieve their development goals. Unfortunately, such media are not always available.

Content

Many elements influence ICT content production in Africa. Most of the content is published, on the Internet in English and to a lesser extent in French. As well, the rate of illiteracy is very high on the continent (about 70% of the population) both in official (mainly English and French) and local languages.

Rural African economies are still in a "pre-market" situation, and most of the information available on the Internet does not necessarily correspond to the needs of rural communities. Sometimes the information is simply not presented in a format that is understandable and accessible to these communities. School communities also face problems when adapting and using Internet content. Even when content is adaptable, its translation into understandable language and presentation in appropriate and affordable formats require technical skills and financial and technical resources that are not always available in the communities concerned.

Study findings revealed that content production and development are very limited. Such is the case of the Msunduzi project, which started with a consultative and participatory process to identify the information to decide on the information to be published on its web site. This site contains information formatted like a newspaper (because of access constraints a paper version is

74

also distributed to reach as many people as possible). In this way, information on environmental matters and rehabilitation measures appropriate for the Msunduzi River environment are distributed in different ways to the target community. In Senegal, under the VCMR project, specific content was developed and released in CD-ROM format. This CD-ROM included specific applications on local governance, resource management, and preventive health that had been developed in Microsoft Access. These examples seem to be isolated cases because many constraints continue to restrict content development: technical constraints include limited numbers of computers and limited human resource capacities; economic constraints include high costs of computer services and content adaptation; and knowledge constraints require answers to questions such as what are the information needs, how can content be adapted to local needs, and in what form should the information be presented? These questions remain unanswered.

New ICTs remain a comparatively recent innovation in most of the countries covered by these studies, especially in rural areas. For rural populations to be able to choose the types of applications, services, and content that they need, they must first become familiar with the technologies and then learn about applications and content that are adapted to their realities and needs. However, because their knowledge of ICTs is still very limited, it is difficult for them to make decisions about content and applications that may be appropriate to their needs.

Within these projects, little concern was given to identifying the changing needs of the populations as they grow more familiar with ICTs. Therefore, information and communication needs must be regularly updated. When development-support organizations become involved in projects, their intervention should focus on the development of relevant local content adapted to community needs.

Technologies

Few countries are capable of radical innovation as R&D becomes more expensive and complicated. For these countries, a more relevant indicator is the capacity, in terms of know-how and wealth, to make the appropriate choice between competing technologies and to develop or adapt alone technology to fit their own needs (Hawkins and Valantin 1997).

In South Africa, Kenya, Uganda, and Senegal basic telecommunication infrastructures (e.g., radio, facsimile, telephone, and television) exists, and many modern technologies are often available (e.g., fibre optic lines, Internet, cellular telephone, satellites, and high capacity data transfer networks). These countries have policies in place to encourage expansion and modernization of telecommunication equipment. The majority also have liberalized telecommunications policies. Whereas, the telecommunications sector was once a state monopoly, it has been liberalized and fierce competition exists between operators. This has contributed to considerable improvements in the technological environment, including an increase in the number of services offered and the introduction of new technologies. The emergence of private operators has led to a steady increase in the use of cellular phones, local private radio stations are growing rapidly, and email use has increased as the number of telecentres has risen.

However, the unique aspect of the Acacia program was that it supported projects in the marginalized areas of these countries. As in many villages and marginalized areas of Africa, the system of communication as well as access to ICTs was deficient. These areas were also lacking in more traditional technologies and services – electricity, water and sanitation systems, radios, and telephones. When the VCMR project was started in Senegal, the sites of Sinthiou Malem and Maka Coulibantang had no power supply and power generators were used to supply electricity. A similar situation was observed in Kenya. The project had to be transferred to another village because to the absence of power frustrated the initial target communities.

In most of the areas where ICTs were introduced under the Acacia program, the people became relatively familiar with the ICTs either by seeing or using them. However, the people still tend to make more use of the available traditional technologies in these areas – radios, telephones, and duplicating machines. The specific contribution of the Acacia program was its support for the introduction of digital technologies (including the Internet) to marginalized rural and suburban areas. As a research program, its purpose was to test the adaptability of these tools to be able to offer African countries a wider range of technological choices. Accordingly, through pilot projects, the communities were given access to different equipment that had been previously unknown to most of the people or only in limited use. Computers and accessories as well as other tools such as CD-ROM and scanners were introduced. ICTs are slowly making their way into the communities. The

Acacia program accelerated the introduction of new technologies. As user needs grew clearer and more sophisticated, new equipment was called for and often supplied. As a result, information and access to equipment became diversified and varied from one area to another and from one site to another.

In the communities surveyed in Kenya, Uganda, and Senegal, the most frequently used technologies are, in order of importance: telephone, word processing, facsimile, email, and Internet. In Kenya, for example, at Makueni and Kakameya, 73% of the people used the telephone compared with only 18% who used the computer for word processing, 18% who used the facsimile machine, and 3% who used email. Nobody reported surfing on the Internet. Also in Uganda, the new ICTs were not used very much (Tables 18–22). The majority of people most frequently use the telephone (58% of those interviewed) and only 6.4% and 9.0% of those surveyed said they had used email and word processing services. Not even one respondent mentioned surfing on the Internet. Apart from the telephone, the facsimile machine is also used, but mainly by people involved in very profitable activities (5.1%).

Widespread use of the telephone was consolidated by the opening of community telecentres by Acacia, mainly on ENDA sites located in the suburbs of Dakar, Senegal. Similarly, in South Africa (Burton 2001), the project brought access to the Internet to communities in Sobantu, Woodlands, Willowfontein, Georgetown, and Vulindlela communities. Therefore, the technical conditions for the extension of ICT use in the communities can be met. The increasing demand for new equipment confirms that there is a capacity to absorb new electronic equipment. Facsimile is widely accepted because it is easy to access (easy to use and low cost), which implies that if new ICTs become very common, available, and ultimately accessible and affordable, they might be used on a larger scale. The use of new ICTs largely depends on their accessibility. Although an operator can assist with the use of a facsimile machine, the use of email requires some skills. This implies that a good command of new ICTs is a prerequisite for their extensive use.

The technologies that have been introduced to date have been generally based on fixed telephone lines. Some studies have looked at technology adaptability (infrastructure and equipment) because Internet access problems continue to be very common in many areas. For example, in Matam, Senegal, users of the youth cyber space spent weeks without access to the Internet (partly because of narrow bandwidth). In Vulindlela, South Africa, the community has frequent connectivity problems that prevent access to the project web site. In some mountainous areas of Uganda, fixed telephone lines are not very common and, therefore, web technology is not widely accessible to communities. The constraints associated with cable technologies suggest that alternative technologies (wireless for example) that can promote widespread access to new ICTs should be pursued. Efforts should also be made to seek mechanisms that combine new technologies with more traditional ones to help meet the needs of the people at the lowest possible cost.

Prerequisites for ICT use

Although significant progress has been observed in the telecommunication infrastructure, major constraints still hinder the promotion of universal access to ICTs. These constraints prevent potential users and communities in areas far from the capital cities from deriving substantial benefits from the use of ICTs. Most of the infrastructure continues to be concentrated in large urban centres. In general, the development of the technological environment provides a significant potential to use ICTs for development purposes. However, in the surveyed rural and suburban areas, telecommunication and economic infrastructures remain inadequate. Of course, sectoral policies and initiatives targeted at specific areas of ICT application do exist in South Africa, Kenya, Uganda, and Senegal. Regulatory bodies have been established, particularly in the context of liberalizing the telecommunications sector (in Senegal the regulating body was established in 2002). However, all these countries lack a consistent, systematic, and integrated ICT policy that reflects the global macro-economic situation in each country. This can both prevent universal access and nullify the benefits expected from ICTs.

Some individuals have managed to use specific ICTs in isolated cases, mainly for electronic trade. However, others, due to financial, institutional, and logistic constraints have been unable to take advantage of these opportunities. This is reflected in the case of the Sinthiou Malem-based commercial venture, Thiané et Frères, in Senegal:

> I know that you can do good business with the Internet, but you need a sound financial position. I learnt this at my own expense when I wanted to buy galvanized wire. Our venture operates a small-sized wire netting unit, and I saw on the Internet a very attractive price offered for galvanized wire (about one third of the selling price in Dakar, all costs included). But, to take advantage of this low price, I would have needed to buy a large quantity. Because I did not have a lot of cash, I could not benefit from this

opportunity. (Statement made by Cheikh Thiané at the Feedback Workshop on ICTs and Community Development, Senegal, July 2001)

The lack of adequate basic infrastructure, such as power supply, is also an impediment. For example, the implementation of the Acacia governance project had to be transferred to another site because of power supply problems. This frustrated the first target community. In Senegal, in the villages of Maka Coulibantang and Sinthiou Malem, which are located far from Dakar, there was no power supply and power generators were used to operate telecentres. This also caused a number of problems such as the high cost of fuel and computer breakdowns caused by power fluctuations. In another example, the lack of proper storage facilities, and inadequate organization among the women, prevented women fish wholesalers in Joal, Senegal, from satisfying the demand of "virtual" customers. The absence of adequate storage facilities for the perishable fish made it impossible for the women to meet the quality and quantity demands of their new customers. Many similar examples attest to the need for a policy and institutional environment that favours democratic access to ICTs and provision of supporting infrastructure. Training in the management of small- and medium-sized businesses is also required. Entrepreneurs must be able to manage their operations and activities to take maximum advantage of the opportunities offered by ICTs. To participate in electronic business, many quality, quantity, and cash requirements must be met

There is also a lack of systematic ICT policy in the countries studied. For example, existing policies limit the institutionalization of ICTs in education in Senegal. A multidimensional approach is required to develop an integrated vision of how ICTs might best be used to support development. Considerations of how to use ICTs for development purposes must be integrated into the existing political, economic, cultural, and social framework.

Table 16: Types of services used at the TPS Unit at Joal, Senegal
(January 1999 to November 2000)

Services Used	Organizations and Institutions	Individual Users		Total
		Women	Men	
Internet navigation	14	41	60	115
Email	43	27	226	296
Word processing	432	18	256	704
Trade registration	12	0	15	27
Advertisements	6	0	3	9
Scanning	1	0	0	1
Faxing	1	0	3	4
Training	0	2	3	5
Total	509	88	565	1162

Source: Thioune and Sène 'Calculations based on database maintained by Joal TPS unit' (2001).

Table 17: Types of services used at Joal (urban area) and Ross-Béthio (rural area) in Senegal (November 2000)

Services Used	Organizations and Institutions		Individual Users				Total
			Women		Men		
	Joal	Ross-Béthio	Joal	Ross-Béthio	Joal	Ross-Béthio	
Internet navigation	14	3	41	0	60	15	133
Email	43	9	27	6	226	53	364
Word processing	432	33	18	1	256	50	788
Trade registration	12	0	0	0	15	4	31
Opportunity ads	6	0	0	0	3	0	9
Scanning	1	0	0	0	0	0	1
Faxing	1	0	0	0	3	0	4
Training	0		2	1	3	0	6
Search for business opportunities	0	0	0	0	0	1	1
Telephone calls	0	21	0	0	0	17	38
Total	509	66	88	8	566	140	1375

Source: Thioune and Sène 'Calculations based on databases maintained by TPS units in Ross-Béthio and Joal in Senegal' (2001).

Table 18: Types of services used in different locations in Uganda (2002)

Region***	Location	Services* (%)					
		Tel.	Fax	Internet	Word processing	Email	Others**
Nakawa	Banda	60.0	40.0	0.0	20.0	0.0	0.0
	Bugolobi	60.0	0.0	0.0	0.0	0.0	20.0
	Bukoto	80.0	20.0	0.0	20.0	40.0	20.0
Nabweru	Kazo-Nabweru	100.0	0.0	0.0	60.0	0.0	40.0
	Manganjo	80.0	0.0	0.0	0.0	0.0	20.0
	Nansana	75.0	0.0	0.0	25.0	0.0	0.0
Buwama	Mbizzinya	66.7	16.7	0.0	16.7	16.7	16.7
	Jalamba	25.0	0.0	0.0	0.0	25.0	0.0
	Katebo	66.7	0.0	0.0	0.0	33.3	66.7
Rubaya	Karujanga	70.0	0.0	0.0	0.0	0.0	30.0
	Kibuga	38.5	0.0	0.0	0.0	0.0	7.7
	Rwanyena	23.1	0.0	0.0	0.0	0.0	0.0

Source : Etta et al. (2001).

Note: * Multiple responses given; ** mainly photocopying; *** regions of Nakawa, Nabweru and Buwama are covered by CEEWA; Rubaya by AHI.

Table 19: Main sources of information on ICTs in Uganda

Information Sources	Answers*	
	Percentage	Number
Radio	69.2	54
Television	23.1	18
Newspapers	20.5	16
Project	12.8	10
NGO	24.4	19
Acacia project	23.1	18
Other	17.9	14

Source: Etta et al. (2001).

Note: * Based on multiple responses.

Table 20: First time ICTs were used in Uganda

	Percentage	Number
Before 1998	35.6	16
1999	20.0	9
2000	44.4	20
Total	100.0	45

Source: Etta et al. (2001).

Table 21: Frequency of use of ICTs in different locations in Uganda (2000)

Region*	Location	Frequency (%)			
		Every day	Every week	Never	Some times
Nakawa	Banda	33.3	0.0	33.3	33.3
	Bugolobi	0.0	0.0	66.7	33.3
	Bukoto	50.0	25.0	0.0	25.0
Nabweru	Kazo-Nabweru	0.0	0.0	0.0	100.0
	Manganjo	0.0	50.0	0.0	50.0
	Nansana	0.0	66.7	0.0	33.3
Buwama	Mbizzinya	50.0	25.0	0.0	25.0
	Jalamba	100.0	0.0	0.0	0.0
	Katebo	0.0	66.7	0.0	33.3
Rubaya	Karujanga	0.0	14.3	0.0	85.7
	Kibuga	0.0	16.7	0.0	83.3
	Rwanyena	0.0	0.0	0.0	100.0

Source: Etta et al. (2001).
Note: * Regions of Nakawa, Nabweru and Buwama are covered by CEEWA; Rubaya by AHI.

Table 22: Reasons for using ICTs in Uganda (2000)

Region*	Location	Work	Contact family members	Trade	Education and research	Agric. info.	health info	Leisure	Others
					Reason (%)				
Nakawa	Banda	0.0	60.0	20.0	0.0	0.0	0.0	0.0	0.0
	Bugolobi	20.0	60.0	0.0	0.0	0.0	0.0	0.0	0.0
	Bukoto	60.0	80.0	20.0	0.0	0.0	0.0	0.0	0.0
Nabweru	Kazo-Nabweru	60.0	80.0	40.0	0.0	0.0	20.0	0.0	0.0
	Manganjo	0.0	40.0	20.0	0.0	0.0	0.0	0.0	0.0
	Nansana	0.0	50.0	50.0	0.0	0.0	0.0	0.0	0.0
Buwama	Mbizzinya	50.0	50.0	16.7	16.7	16.7	16.7	0.0	0.0
	Jalamba	25.0	25.0	0.0	25.0	0.0	0.0	0.0	0.0
	Katebo	66.7	100.0	33.3	33.3	0.0	0.0	0.0	0.0
Rubaya	Karujanga	50.0	70.0	10.0	20.0	0.0	0.0	0.0	100.0
	Kibuga	23.1	30.8	0.0	0.0	0.0	0.0	0.0	0.0
	Rwanyena	7.7	15.4	0.0	0.0	0.0	0.0	0.0	0.0
Moyenne		28.2	48.7	12.8	6.4	1.3	2.6	3.8	2.6

Source: Etta et al. (2001).

Note: * Regions of Nakawa, Nabweru, Mbizzinya and Buwama are covered by CEEWA; Rubaya by AHI.

Conclusion

The fact that ICTs are increasingly integrated into the development programs of African countries is confirmed by their prominent position in the New Partnership for Africa's Development (NEPAD). Steps are being taken to gradually institutionalize ICT tools in the economic and social system of African countries to promote more rapid integration of these countries into the information economy. However, Chapter 2 of this study shows that these steps are still limited and that general strategies or policies that integrate ICTs into the global macro-economic framework of these countries are lacking. Integration of African nations into the information economy will require far-reaching actions that will affect all aspects of economic and social life. However, the potential exists for ICTs to be used in all fields of activity if the constraints limiting their transforming effects can be lifted.

The main objective of this study was not to assess Acacia's assumption that African communities can find new ways to improve their living conditions with ICTs. However, research has shown that ICTs, and particularly the new ICTs, can contribute to improving the living conditions of African populations. ICTs can make this contribution by helping to meet the dynamic and changing expectations of Africans for access to information on such subjects as agriculture, education, and governance. As people become familiar with ICTs, they discover the opportunities that these tools can offer and express their needs on the basis of the anticipated usefulness of these technologies. In other words, they anticipate the capacity of ICTs to deliver information that will solve the practical and concrete problems they face. As demonstrated in Chapter 4, the communities have undergone substantial changes in their effort to appropriate the tools. The changes, which have occurred at the individual level and within community organizations, include capacity building, acquisition of new skills, more efficiency in community activities, and better integration of previously marginalized groups. Therefore, it is urgent to take far-reaching actions to meet not only expectations but also to consolidate the advances that have been made in ICT appropriation by these African communities.

This research identified several challenges and problems that were common to the countries studied. However, most of these challenges and problems affect the whole of Africa. The challenges must be faced by the communities themselves, researchers, and decision-making bodies (states as well as research and development financing institutions). Generally, these challenges relate to participation and ICT appropriation mechanisms and to materials and formats that can be used to collect, organize, disseminate, and share useful information and knowledge using ICTs. Other challenges include: the availability of adequate formal and informal training in, and with, ICTs; the establishment of an institutional framework that favours the use of ICTs for development purposes; and the provision of democratic access to ICTs for all community members.

The following recommendations suggest actions that can help ensure that ICTs serve the development needs of Africa.

1. There is no single way of introducing ICTs. The process is dynamic and consists of several stages in Africa. The first stage consists of raising awareness about the potential of ICTs for community development. The second stage is to encourage basic use of ICTs. The third stage consists of providing specific products and content to meet local demands (e.g., materials in national languages and products tailored to the needs of specific sectors of the population, such as disabled people). This is a challenging situation for researchers and development organizations, which must be able to adjust to the pace of increasing community needs. Political decision-makers are also affected by these challenges because they must set up legal and regulatory frameworks that create the optimum conditions for equal access and appropriation of ICTs within and by communities

2. Participation is a crucial problem in the process of introducing and promoting the use of ICTs for community development. In the communities surveyed, ICTs were generally introduced through projects and community participation was often limited to complementary contributions. The research findings demonstrate that appropriation mechanisms have been initiated within the communities, but finding ways to involve large segments of the population still constitutes a real problem, even when people are aware of the potential usefulness of ICTs. In-depth studies must be carried out to understand the decision-making mechanisms of the different community actors with regard to ICTs. It is equally important to try to better understand the attitude of communities toward changes, so as to identify the factors that underlie the adoption of ICTs by poor rural communities.

The research revealed that negative external factors (e.g., inequality and discrimination) are associated with the process of introducing ICTs. Such factors must be identified and taken into consideration when seeking to encourage the use of ICTs to support equitable, harmonious, and well-balanced development. The access of poor communities to ICTs seems to be determined by several factors (e.g., site, income, sex, age, language, and education level). However, more systematic studies and in-depth analyses based on data collected over a long period are needed to identify the kind, type, and sense of the relationships between ICT use for development and these different factors. With such studies, it should also be possible to determine the relationship between the use of ICTs and the different factors that are identified. Such analyses and study seems to be most relevant when confined to a homogeneous geographical area such as a country.

3. One of the major research findings of this study is that women barely use ICTs, and when they do women use these tools less than men, even when they are relatively literate. Knowing that women's involvement, despite some resistance and constraints, is a prerequisite for their participation in the information economy, steps should be taken to promote some kind of positive discrimination toward women. In terms of future plans and interventions, projects specifically designed for women seem to offer efficient ways to obtain this involvement. Women's involvement in project management and the promotion of leadership by women, are also important conditions for enhancing their participation and appropriation of ICTs. Research should also be conducted to find information media tools and applications adapted to women's conditions, needs, and roles in the community, and to their mode of thinking (Rathgeber 2000). Such research could help minimize the socio-cultural constraints that limit access by women to ICTs.

4. As a rule, the technologies that were introduced were adapted to the limited infrastructure available at the study sites. However, due to installation costs and the recurrent expenses involved in the use of new technologies (i.e., Internet and email), alternative technologies (e.g., satellites with wireless technology and multimedia tools) could be used in future projects to improve community access. The number of

community access points could also be increased to combine the more familiar traditional technologies with the new ICTs.

5. Adaptable and affordable alternative technologies are needed to ensure universal access to ICTs. In light of the findings of this research, one can affirm that ICTs can actually contribute to improving the living conditions of the populations. It is necessary to assess the amount of real change and to identify and evaluate the effects that ICT use have on income levels (both for individuals and the community). Knowing that income is an important factor in the evaluation of individual and community standards of living, further research based on real experiences is needed to better understand and measure the economic impact of ICTs on poverty reduction and wealth production.

6. Due to country specificity and the importance of institutional context to ICT project implementation, national approaches should be encouraged to study the use of ICTs for development purposes. A national institutional environment seems to be a relevant framework for conducting studies on ICTs and development.

Appendix 1

Evaluation and Learning System for Acacia (ELSA–Acacia)[1]

Acacia's basic assumption is that by using ICTs, poor communities in Africa can contribute more efficiently to their own development and avoid or go rapidly through the traditional stages of the development process. This hypothesis is tested under the Acacia project activity.

Learning and experimentation are important characteristics of the Acacia approach to development and to the adoption of ICTs in developing communities. This approach is reflected in the very design of the initiative, in its participatory strategy as well as in the integration of evaluation and learning in all stages of project implementation. Therefore, the evaluation component of the Acacia initiative goes beyond assessing the objectives and results achieved. It is an evaluation approach that combines continuous learning and experimentation within its analysis. It is essential that changes that occur be based on lessons drawn, either from within the Initiative per se, from that of Acacia partners or from the development context as a whole.

The key learning mechanisms include self-evaluations and the partners to the Initiative, the participants and project staff working in harmony to determine learning objectives and to work out a common understanding of the results achieved under an Acacia activity. This implies setting up feedback mechanisms, allocating resources to guide and train participants and exchange opportunities between the different partners to the initiative.

---

[1] Source: http://network.idrc.ca/ev.php?url_id=5906&do=do_topic

The formulae adopted by the Evaluation and Learning System for Acacia (ELSA) is innovative per se as it covers persistent learning and evaluation as well as new knowledge and what is imbibed is transmitted both to Acacia managers and to the communities directly.

Exchanges with the main Acacia partners constitute an integral part of ELSA, so that their own views on the criteria for an effective approach and the standard to report the progress and results achieved could be incorporated in the permanent learning and evaluation framework. The Acacia program will, as much as possible, facilitate ELSA's work through electronic connectivity. Paving the way, IDRC has published on its web site the reports and studies related to each of the phases of the Initiative. Furthermore, the "Exchanges with Acacia" section was created in an initial effort to stimulate information flows to the Initiative thus encouraging a two-way interaction.

Evaluation and learning take place at all levels of the Acacia Initiative and this is so not only to be able to assess the impact of Acacia on community life or the relevance, efficiency and visibility of its various projects and programs, but also to understand the role and effects of ICTs on project behaviour (and project participants') and on the achievement of project objectives. For further details on the impact of ICTs on development aid, check out the site Learning and Action Program (GK–LEAP) web site run by Bellanet, one of Acacia's partners.

The ELSA approach consists of four integrated components:

1.   Project evaluations aimed at collecting reference data and assessing programs in accordance with the needs of IDRC and other parties to the Initiative.
2.   Use of innovating ICT mechanisms and tools to promote learning and feedback at all levels.
3.   Research to test hypotheses derived from knowledge acquired through the Acacia Initiative.
4.   Exchanges at all levels between parties to the Acacia Initiative to ensure that lessons derived from projects are disseminated, adapted, and then fed back into the program activity and implementation.

Appendix 2

Description of Projects

1. A Community-Based Electronic Environmental Network in the Msunduzi River Catchment[2]

The Msunduzi River catchment covers an area of 540 km^2 and contains over 500,000 people, 400,000 of whom live in the urban and peri-urban area of Pietermaritzburg-Msunduzi. The balance live predominantly in the rural area of Vulindlela which forms the upper catchment. A great many of the people living in the catchment come from disadvantaged backgrounds, are poorly educated, and have limited understanding of environmental and development issues. This, combined with inappropriate development and land use by administrative and management authorities and commercial and industrial interests, has caused a significant decline in the environmental health of the catchment. The poor environmental health contributes towards social instability, and also apathy towards the environment. Conversely, good environmental health can contribute towards a sense of belonging, community pride and social stability, as well as reducing community health problems.

Together with the Department of Water Affairs and Forestry (DWAF), Umgeni Water had earlier embarked on the Mgeni Catchment Management Plan of which the Msunduzi Catchment forms a part. This initiative identified

---

[2] Extract from 'A Community-Based Electronic Environmental Network in the Msunduzi River Catchment: A Review and a Model.' Paper Prepared for the Acacia Project by Nick Rivers-More and Duncan Hay, Institute of Natural Resources, August 1998.

the following key issues in the Msunduzi Catchment (related to water quality and quantity):

- High levels of faecal contamination indicating that water supply and sanitation systems (including educational systems) are inadequate.
- High levels of sediment entering storage dams indicating high rates of soil erosion caused by inappropriate land use and civil engineering practices.
- High levels of phosphorous caused by industrial discharge and run-off from cultivated land.
- Metal contamination caused mainly by industry and motor vehicles.
- Aquatic health declining because of the invasion of alien riparian (riverine) vegetation, pollution and natural habitat destruction.
- Flooding periodically accounting for a number of lives and livelihoods.

A short walk in the Azalea area of Greater Edendale is sufficient to bring into stark reality the problems people face. Gashes of soil erosion caused by over-grazing; external pit latrines oozing raw sewerage into adjacent streams; smashed standpipes spewing thousands of gallons of water into storm-water drains; formal homes constructed within flood risk areas, or directly in wetlands and stream-beds; cuts and fills of a construction site with no rehabilitating vegetation covering them; litter in all conceivable forms strewn along the riverbanks; and of greatest concern, the number of people unemployed and at home.

One of the keys to addressing these issues is improving the understanding of those whose actions impact on the environment – not only the poor but also industrialists, developers and city administrators. A lack of knowledge on relevant issues can lead to poor environmental health and/or an inability to rectify the problem. Conversely, information "overload" can be overwhelming without the necessary guidance on how to filter out the relevant information in order to use the knowledge to improve environmental quality. People from all socio-economic sectors need to understand the consequences of their actions. Only through this will people modify their behaviour towards the environment. The basis for improved understanding is access to information and increased interaction between and within socio-economic levels and sectors. (The Greater Edendale Environmental Network and the Institute of Natural Resources held a community-based workshop with about 50 participants in Pietermaritzburg-Msunduzi recently. The objective was to introduce community leaders to the concept of Integrated Catchment Management and to establish a common vision for the catchment. The community leaders cited a lack of information as one of the major constraints to effective environmental management of the catchment.) For the vast majority of people, gaining access to information and interacting through formal education on environment and development issues is not a realistic option. Gaining knowledge and understanding that allows people to make informed decisions on their lives and the environment has to take a different and less formal route. "Local–Local" dialogue–interaction and the exchange of information – between community groups, between community groups and experts, and between community groups, NGOs and government (local, provincial and national) – is essential so that different perspectives are understood and all parties are empowered to take decisions and act effectively.

The historical roots of this programme go back to 25 December 1995, where the need for improved information management and communication in a catchment context was spurred by the floods of Christmas Day 1995. This flood devastated areas of the catchment, killed 160 people and displaced over 500 families. All of these people were settled in flood risk areas. This disaster illustrated graphically to what extent marginalized and disadvantaged people have been separated from environmental processes. A general lack of comprehension and understanding of the danger of settling on floodplains, a lack of opportunities to settle elsewhere, a deteriorating catchment and an episodic rainfall event formed a highly lethal combination. While a project was initiated to provide short-term solutions to the flooding – simply to identify those living in areas of extreme risk and move them – there was the general recognition that a more holistic catchment management approach was required, in order to solve the multifaceted problems that exist in the catchment. With funds donated by the GTZ Rural Development Foundation, four organizations teamed up to commence the Msunduzi Integrated Catchment Management Initiative. They were:

- Institute of Natural Resources (INR)
- Greater Edendale Environmental Network (GREEN)
- Computing Centre for Water Research (CCWR)
- Share-Net

Activities in this initiative included:

- Establishing a conceptual and contextual basis for achieving sustainable development in the Msunduzi Catchment.
- Compiling a data base of catchment stakeholders.
- Setting up a catchment management "leadership group."
- Developing a common vision amongst stakeholders of what the desired state of the catchment might be and how this might be achieved.
- Being actively involved in community-based initiatives so as to achieve an improved understanding of catchment based problems.
- Formulating of information management and education strategies.
- Developing, through these initiatives, an Integrated Catchment Management strategy for the whole catchment.

In investigating this approach the critical role of communication and effective information transfer became apparent. The opinion was expressed that if disadvantaged communities gained access to catchment-based information relevant to their lives and livelihoods it would place them in a better position to respond. One way of creating, sharing and accessing information is through the Internet. There is general agreement that for any catchment-based activity to be successful effective communication and co-creation of information is vitally critical. The sharing of information, and co-ordination of actions based on that information between and within sectors and levels of society, is also important. A specific issue is access to relevant information by, and effective communication with, organisations that represent the various communities resident in the catchment. So as to address this, the INR, with technical and conceptual support from the CCWR, commenced with a pilot project in establishing three electronic communication and information centres within or linked to communities, and operated by a community-based organization:

- Indumiso Environmental Awareness Society (IEAS);
- Greater Edendale Environmental Network (GREEN); and
- Sobantu Environmental Desk.

Success was mixed, but progress has been made in the following areas:

- Training in computer skills and electronic networking is taking place.
- IEAS and GREEN have established their own web sites.
- GREEN has compiled its own newsletter located on the home page and also distributed it as hardcopy to community representatives.
- Both groups are interacting regularly with institutions and accessing information off the Internet.
- Feedback from the various activities that the groups carry out in the catchment area is also fed into their web sites.
- Sections of the computer-based Integrated Catchment Information System (ICIS) have been loaded on to the IEAS computer and members are inputting and manipulating data collected on field trips.
- Establishment of the Sobantu site has commenced.

There is a fundamental need to increase the number of sites and to encourage other initiatives/organizations to fund their own sites so as to increase the flow of information to and from community groups and to improve communication. There is also a need to formulate, test and refine a communication and information-sharing model for broad catchment-based application. This is where this project is relevant, in that it aims to increase the number of sites from where knowledge sharing can take place. Although the project is aimed at the residents of peri-urban and urban areas it is important to include also those rural residents in the upper catchment. Their activities impact on the urban environment downstream and so their participation in the project process is critical.

Project goal and objectives

The goal of this project was to improve decision making through effective communication and information management on environment and development issues among communities and institutions in the Msunduzi River catchment. The specific project objectives were as follow:

1. Review the international, national and local experiences of community-based communication and information systems.

97

2. Expand community-based electronic network in the Msunduzi River Catchment (from three to eight hubs) and operate effectively as a medium for improving environmental decision-making.
3. Establish GREEN as an effective central hub in the electronic network.
4. Train representatives of participating organizations to be computer literate and to able to effectively network electronically.
5. Make representatives of participating organizations aware of environmental and development issues and their consequences and able to jointly take decisions to resolve these issues.
6. Support representatives of participating organizations in transferring their understanding of environment and development issues to the broader community.
7. Ensure that information on environment and development issues in the Msunduzi River catchment are consolidated, accessible and understandable to communities.
8. Formulate, test and validate electronic information and communication model that focuses on community groups, which can be applied broadly at local and regional level and that informs a national strategy.
9. Evaluate the project effectively.
10. Plan, develop and fund ongoing networking activities.

2. Enhancing women's participation in governance through increased access to civic information

This project, which commenced in 1998, is being implemented by the Family Support Institute, (FASI) Kenya. FASI is a local NGO working in rural communities in parts of the country and especially with women on family health issues. FASI identified two centres for the implementation and operation of the project, namely: Shibuye location in Kakamega District, Western province and Nguumo location in Makueni District of the Eastern Province.

The main objective of the project is to build on existing infrastructure in community-based resource centres, to provide women from the two rural communities of Kakamega and Makueni with the ability to access, generate and utilize civic information to enhance their participation in governance. The resource centres were to be used to perform functions similar to those of telecentres.

98

It is expected that through this project, women's awareness of their civic rights and responsibilities in the project locations at least will be heightened and a pool of informed women who can intelligently participate in the electoral process created. Accountability and transparency, constituents of good governance, will be deepened among women through their involvement in continuous civic education programmes provided within the project using ICTs.

It is also expected that at the conclusion of this project, women's capacity to participate in political decision-making and especially in matters related to their development would have improved. This would have been made possible through the use of ICTs in the expansion and upgrading of their traditional information systems and networks.

Specific objectives

- To increase women's awareness of their civic rights and responsibilities
- Increase the pool of informed women who can participate in the electoral process as candidates and voters.
- Increase women's representation in decision-making positions in public and private sectors.
- Increase control of the electoral process by community members and promote the principles of free and fair elections.
- Create awareness of the virtues of accountability, transparency and good governance.
- Improve community women's capacity for decision-making relating to development by increasing their access to Information Communication Technologies (ICTs), and their ability to use them for their own needs
- Create increased opportunities for communities to update their information on governance.
- Provide increased opportunities for communities to use ICTs to upgrade their traditional information systems and networks.

Project activities

The activities of the project and the resource or telecentres were identified as follows:

- Undertaking needs assessment in the project target districts to determine the status of civic information resources and information and communication technologies.

- Convening a consultative meeting for stakeholders to review and share information on existing civic materials and information and communication technology resources, assess their adequacy, identify gaps and develop an action plan.
- Generating additional civic education materials and secure information and communication technologies and establish a training programme responding to the identified needs.
- Establishing resource centres in both project areas equipped with comprehensive civic educational materials and information and communication technologies and training programmes.
- Recruiting resource people skilled in information and communication technologies, retainers skilled in management of community resource centres and women group leaders from communities in the target areas to participate in the project.
- Providing training for retainers, and volunteer trainers who will be women group leaders in the management and use of community-based information centres and information and communication technologies.
- Training women group members from the local communities in civic education and management and use of community-based information centres and information and communication technologies.
- Organizing exchange tours between women from different areas to share information.

3. Economic empowerment of women through ICTs

This Acacia project in Uganda is supported by IDRC as a pilot initiative in the country aimed at empowering poor rural communities to improve their socio-economic conditions and acquire capacity to address their local needs through the use of modern ICTs. This project is intended to maximize the use of telecentre projects through establishing complementary applications useful to rural community needs such as telemedicine, electronic delivery of agricultural information and equipping women entrepreneurs with information and skills.

Background

The Council for the Economic Empowerment of Women of Africa (CEEWA) – Uganda Chapter is a non-profit organization that was set up with the explicit objective of promoting the economic empowerment of women in the development process. In order to address women's concerns, CEEWA-Uganda has adopted a number of strategies, which include:

- Training and sensitisation.
- Research and documentation.
- Lobbying for participation in relevant technical committees and task forces commissioned by mainstream economy-related organizations.
- Participation in collaborative lobbying and advocacy initiatives with other NGOs.

In implementing the above strategies, CEEWA-Uganda has put in place four major programmes, namely:
- Women and Economic Decision-Making. This programme brings together women professionals in various multidisciplinary fields to work as a group in mainstreaming women's concerns in the economic development process.
- Women and Finance. This programme aims at strengthening and enhancing gender equity in micro-finance initiatives.
- Resource Centre Project. The overall objective of this programme is to strengthen and enhance the use of information and communication technologies by women and their organizations.
- Women and Agriculture. The primary objective of this programme is to support Government and NGOs in developing agricultural extension services deliverable in a gender responsive manner.

Project objectives

In line with its overall goal – of increasing women's access to and control of economic resources – CEEWA-Uganda is implementing a 2-year project that puts special focus on the use of Information and Communication Technologies (ICTs) to promote the growth and development of women enterprises. The overall objective of the project is to enable women entrepreneurs and women's organisations that promote enterprise development

101

to explore ways and means of exploiting ICTs for community economic empowerment. The project specifically:

- Identify the information needs of micro- and small-scale women entrepreneurs and women organizations in three project sites of Buwama, Nabweru, and Kampala.
- Build human resource capacity, among participating women entrepreneurs and women organisations, through training in entrepreneurship development and ICT application in entrepreneurship.
- Establish a Women Information Resource and Electronic Services (WIRES) centre that will enable women entrepreneurs to access information relevant to the development of their entrepreneurial skills and the expansion of their existing enterprises.
- Monitor, evaluate, and document the performance of the participating women entrepreneurs and women organizations, and to disseminate the knowledge generated.

4. African Highlands Eco-Regional Program (AHI)

African Highlands Eco-Regional Program (AHI) is a collaborative research program focusing on natural resource management (NRM) in the highlands of East and Central Africa. The project aims at strengthening agricultural research in East and Central Africa, and contributing to the development of communities vis-à-vis sustainable use of natural resources through usage and application of ICTs and other communication approaches in the community. It is envisaged that the ICTs and new approaches will enable farmers to access relevant information from agricultural researchers, extension workers, traders and support agents.

The goal of this project was to contribute to development of communities and the sustainability of natural resources in the intensively cultivated highlands of Eastern Africa through the application and management of ICTs and traditional communication media. The overall purpose of the project was to help farmers increase their knowledge and understanding of technological options in order to make better decisions at household and community levels so that they can produce and market effectively and sustainably skills in NRM.

Project objectives

- Increase farmers and stakeholders technological and market (and other) knowledge and understanding in the use of ICTs so that they can produce and market effectively.
- Motivate and create a capacity of communities to apply and utilize ICTs to meet their expressed needs with respect to production and marketing information.
- Set-up, support the development of the telecentre network and identify the most effective combination of ICTs, which can be applied to enhance farmers' knowledge and skills in NRM and ensure the sustainability of the network.
- Understand the communication process and dynamics in the target communities and assess the factors (positive and negative) affecting the utilization of ICTs for development.

5. Experimentation with Youth Cyber spaces in Intermediate and Secondary Education in Senegal

Senegal is a Sahelian country with a high population growth rate (2.7% annually compared with 0.9% annually in Canada) and a severely deteriorating environment. Its population doubled within 25 years with a very important youth component. About 58% of the population is less than 20 years of age compared with only 5% of elderly people (60 years and above). In a context of premature sexuality, this segment is most vulnerable to the consequences of fecundity and to the progression of AIDS. Surveys on youth sexuality revealed that more than 50% of young school goers experienced sex with no information whatsoever on related risks.

One must confess that the structures involved in advocating for the promotion of reproductive health, the improvement of the environment in which the young mature, and better management of their economic and social development have not seriously consider young people. As part of efforts to find solutions to these problems, GEEP in partnership with the Ministry of National Education, has embarked on a teenage education program designed to inform on problems and issues around population. In this connection, a program on the promotion of training in family life and environmental issues was set up for intermediate and secondary education in Senegal. Its goal was to raise awareness among the youth and to influence their behavioural changes in matters relating to sexual and reproductive health issues.

The target group are (13 and 12 years) pupils and teachers of intermediate and secondary education. GEEP's strategy was to establish Family Life Education (FLE) clubs in these schools to serve as a communication space where there is a permanent dialogue about teenagers' concerns on reproductive health, environment and sustainable development. The number of FLE clubs in schools and universities both in urban and rural areas increased from 73 in July 1996 to 130 in March 1998. The network consists of 1,500 *leaders-pupils-coordinators (LPC)* and 500 *teachers-relays-techniques (TRT)*.

Family Life Education (FLE) clubs are expanding in a context characterized by very strong demand for information, experience sharing and contacts among young people. On the other hand, the growing number of clubs and their dispersion over a vast geographic area make communication increasingly difficult between the GEEP executive team based in Dakar and the FLE clubs. In order to improve this situation, it became clear that it was useful to experiment with the use of ICTs during the second FLE club festival on the theme 'FLE clubs at the Dawn of the twenty-first century,' through the establishment of a youth cyber space with the participation of pupils who demonstrated great innovating and ICT appropriation capacities.

Following the positive results achieved through this experiment, it was recommended that youth cyber spaces are created to assist in improving the learning, facilitation and communication model. A dozen of youth cyber spaces was thus tested nationally through the club network. This process will help to capitalize and develop their achievements, to promote the distant use of the interdisciplinary population teaching model, to assess the impacts of introducing ICTs in club activities to a wider section of the community, and to consolidate information sharing between the clubs, on the one hand, and with Canada 2/3 Youth Club on the other.

Overall objective

Experimentation provides for improving the learning, facilitation and awareness model implemented by FLE clubs and to apply it on population, environmental and sustainable development issues through the introduc-

104

tion of ICTs and the use of youth cyber spaces in intermediate and secondary education in Senegal.

Specific objectives

- to establish twelve (12) youth cyber spaces in the national FLE club network in Senegal;
- to enhance and to capitalize FLE clubs' achievement and to establish an information sharing network between the FLE clubs network and Canada 2/3 Youth;
- to develop the community exposure capacities of FLE clubs;
- to promote the distant use of the interdisciplinary population teaching model; and
- to assess the impact of access to ICTs through FLE club activity and the higher school performance of the pupils.

6. Use and appropriation of new Information and Communication Technologies by community organizations in Senegal

With poverty spreading as a result of the combination of several internal and external factors linked to structural adjustment policies and State withdrawal, popular dynamics are getting organized in urban and suburban areas around such objectives as would improve and help manage the increasingly difficult living conditions of various underprivileged groups. By developing the so-called popular economy, these organizations are becoming gradually autonomous and willing to build their strategic and operational capacities so that they will be able to influence the course of events and be directly involved in matters relating them.

However, the absence of community organizations from standard communication channels limits considerably the scope and impacts of their development actions, which are confined locally and for a fixed period. For this reason, these organizations have been developing communication strategies and have started gradually, in some cases, to take advantage of the resources and opportunities offered by new ICTs.

With this project aimed at reinforcing popular dynamics, a formative research-action methodology is implemented in order to enable the organizations concerned to use these technologies and to appropriate them durably and socially over a network of community resource centres run by them.

Overall objective

Project objective is to build the operational and strategic capacities of community organizations by using and appropriating ICTs through a coordinated network of community resource centres run by groups of local actors.

Specific objectives

- making local actors participate effectively through a research-action-training process (RAT) at all stages of programming, decision-making, implementation and evaluation of actions related to the use and appropriation of ICTs by these groups;
- building capacities within Ecopole to manage the network and provide technical assistance to local actors;
- building technical skills within community groups participating in RAT;
- identifying and developing communal economy resources held by the groups;
- experimenting with community resources centres in eight sites located in extremely poor urban and suburban areas in Dakar;
- undertaking a participatory evaluation of the process, tools and results achieved in order to assess their real impact on the capacities of target community organizations.

7. Introduction of ICTs to the management and rehabilitation of village communities

The region of Tambacounda extends over an area representing one-third of the Senegalese territory and is endowed with significant pastoral, hydro-agricultural, forestry and mining potentials. Because of the quality and spread of its land area and relatively good rainfall, the region offers an alternative area for intensive agriculture and a migration route from the now over-cultivated groundnut basin whose productivity is decreasing. Despite the region's potentials, grassroots communities experience an extremely fragile economic, sanitary and social situation, making the region one of the poorest in the country.

Land-locked villages and their extreme dispersion make things worse for a region which is already short of communications infrastructures, in particular, considerably raising the costs of development programmes, with negative repercussions on economic activities including market access for products on fairly attractive conditions. In order to remedy this situation, WARF (West Africa Rural Foundation) has assisted since 1993 GADEC (Groupe d'Action pour le Développement Communautaire) in defining and implementing a program on village soil management and rehabilitation (PRGTV). GTV's strategy is based on a comprehensive and collective approach to the constraints and opportunities specific to a rural area aiming at a sustainable management of its local resources and basing its interventions on dialogue between all parties, analysing the complexity of and interactions between natural and socio-political phenomena and integration of development activities.

The development challenges faced by the region include, to a large extent, giving the rural populations and their elect access to means of information and communication. In fact, the geographic configuration of local villages and weak or non existent public and private mass media in some places (radio, in particular) have induced processes preventing grassroots communities from consolidating their autonomy, acquiring knowledge, interacting with political authorities and other development partners or developing their external trade relations.

For all these reasons, the region of Tambacounda is an exceptional socio-geographic framework for experimenting, validating or reformulating Acacia basic hypotheses on grassroots community's access to ICTs as one way of ensuring their own development. It is in this framework that WARF and GADEC offered to experiment Acacia strategy in the context of village soil management. The idea is to lead actions encouraging the use of ICTs and to evaluate its impact on the state and modes of managing village resources, and more generally, on the economic and socio-educational activities of the rural populations while also validating parameters in terms of innovation

107

acceptability and appropriation by the different actors. The approach will be based on the participatory development methodologies of the technologies and include training activity and production of tools that actors involved in the implementation of Acacia strategy in Senegal can use.

Overall objective

To lead activities encouraging the use of ICTs and assessing its impacts on the state and modes of managing village resources, on the economic and socio-educational activities of the populations while also validating parameters in terms of innovation acceptability and appropriation by the different actors.

Specific objectives

- **Focus 1:** to carry out participatory studies/analyses on community in-formation and communication system in three village sites covered by the VCMR/DG program; and
- to work out a pattern for these information and communication systems in relation to the State and to the mode of managing village resources.
- **Focus 2:** to identify and to choose collectively the technological solu-tions likely to lift the information and communication constraints faced by the local populations; and
- to analyse and to assess the impact resulting from the introduction of these technologies on the state and modes of managing villages resources.
- **Focus 3:** to analyse the various political, economic, soc,al and cultural parameters likely to influence the process of introducing the technolo-gies and to evaluate their relative importance in observed changes;and
- to devise and propose a method of establishing the concepts on infor-mation and communication systems combining a range of technologies (new, classical and traditional) adapted to rural needs and situation.
- **Focus 4:** to initiate about thirty members of the consultative framework put in place under the Acacia project to participatory concepts and tools for: a diagnosis of a community information and communication system in a rural environment; negotiated and planned introduction of ICTs in rural communities; and evaluation of community projects and programs.

108

Expected results

Based on the basic problem defined under the Acacia project, that is the access of grassroots communities to ICTs, the global results expected from the project inlude the following:

- explaining a range of phenomena linked to the processes of introducing ICTs in the programming framework of village resource management;
- defining a community information and communication system (CIC) concept conceived on the basis of technologies combining appropriate traditional and modern resources adapted to the rural situation;
- producing and disseminating methodological guides, manuals, articles and audiovisual materials informing on experimentation areas and sta-ges. At the same time, the Acacia-GTV project, in accordance with the orientations defined under the transversal consultation mechanism set up by Acacia, proposes to partners learning experience of participatory methodology with rural communities;
- initiating about thirty members of the Acacia consultative framework to participatory methodologies for studies/diagnosis on the constraints and negotiation of development program with rural communities.

8. ICTs and decentralization of Trade Point (TPS) Senegal

In the globalized economy era, largely spurred by the unprecedented development of ICTs, competitiveness becomes a fundamental stake for country growth. It is in this context that the Senegal IX Orientation Plan for Economic and Social Development (1996-2001), stressed both competitiveness and sustainable human development aims to achieving high growth rates while preserving development capacities.

But like the majority of the countries in the sub-region, Senegal has long been protected against international competition through protectionist policies. The current dynamics of the world economy are forcing the country to reinforce competition in its national economy and to develop co-operation with its foreign partners. Accordingly, it must continue to liberalise, to deregulate, to open up its borders and to restructure its production system,

As the national environment plays a central role in competitiveness, its analysis revealed that many factors currently hinder the creation of comparative advantages. These factors include excess regulation of trade procedures, spatial imbalance between Dakar and the provinces, scattered sources of information and information unreliability. This is why national economy actors seized the opportunities afforded by the UNCTAD program on trade efficiency to join the world Trade Points network, which offer various services through ICTs to users (procedure facilitation centre, access point to world trade information and guidance and assistance centre for trade efficiency).

The self-assigned mission of Trade Point Senegal is to promote Senegalese exports, to rationalize imports and to attract foreign investors. This mission is particularly relevant if it covers Senegal as a whole. The Trade Point decentralization project was initiated from this perspective.

The mission assigned to decentralization is to implement policy giving local economic units access to TPS products and services so that they can take maximum useful advantage of the opportunities offered by globalization. This requires establishing on a large-scale a network of community units endowed with the new ICTs at four levels:

1. regional units located at the different levels of local authorities: regions, districts and rural communities;
2. registered telecentres in each region that will would bring the neighbourhood closer together by allowing access to TPS services even to the places of residence entrepreneurs;
3. transmission points based near the headquarters of socio-professional organizations; and
4. international units lodged with Senegal diplomatic missions.

The establishment of this network is expected to boost domestic trade, to improve trade balance, to attract foreign investors, and to popularize the use of the new ICTs.

Overall objective

To experiment decentralization of the services provided by Trade Point Senegal to economic units operating in places outside Dakar, the capital, by using ICTs through a network of community units found at different levels of the local authorities, in two regions of the country.

Specific objectives

*   to identify and select pilot sites to host community units;
*   to make a participatory diagnosis of the socio-economic context of pilot sites and to identify the needs and expectations of local economic units;
*   to determine the configuration and functions of community units so as to test their operational modes in different local contexts;
*   to draw up a strategy and a plan for ensuring the viability of community units;
*   to evaluate the experimental phase with a view to extending community units to other sites across the country;
*   to extend decentralization to other regions.

Expected results

*   making rural populations access national and international information at the same level and time as urban populations;
*   improving the trade performance of rural producers and informal sector entrepreneurs. With the possibility of joining the network, producers located in the inner provinces (arts and crafts workers, women's and youth economic groupings, etc.) can advertise their production inside and outside Senegal;
*   reinforcing actions to promote arts and crafts workers and rural economic units, in general: by allowing access to better supply sources and ensuring quality training, Trade Point will contribute to creating a Senegal trade mark for good quality production. This quality of goods (standards, finishing and packaging) will be decisive for national foreign trade policy. In this connection, Trade Point Senegal envisages developing intensive promotion of home-made products through virtual trade fairs organized over the Internet;
*   stabilizing rural migration or even reversing the trend thanks to the emergence of new rural entrepreneurs.

Bibliography

Acacia, 1997, 'Acacia Strategy Senegal. Report Prepared for IDRC/Acacia Initiative,' Dakar, Senegal. (http://www.idrc.ca/acacia/outputs/op-seng.htm)

Achia, R., 2000, *Communication to the Subsistence Farmer: An Overview of Possible Methods, Tools and Media*. A Working Paper, Food and Agriculture Organization of the United Nations (FAO), Kampala, Uganda.

Adam, L. and Wood, F., 1999, 'An Investigation of the Impact of Information and Communication Technologies in Sub-Saharan Africa.' *Journal of Information Science,* 25(4), 307-318.

Adeya, N., 2001, *Information and Communication Technologies in Africa: A Review and Selective Annotated Bibliography.* (http://www.inasp.org.uk/pubs/ict/index.html)

Agonga, A., 2000 'A Report of the Pan-African Study on Information and Communication Technologies and Community Development.' IDRC, Nairobi, Kenya (December, unpublished).

Asingwire, N., 2001, 'An Evaluation Study of Economic Empowerment of Women Through ICTs and AHI – Acacia Projects in Uganda.' IDRC, Nairobi, Kenya (April, unpublished).

Bhatnagar, S., 2000, 'Social Implications of Information and Communication Technology in Developing Countries: Lessons from Asian Success Stories.' *The Electronic Journal on Information Systems in Developing Countries,* Volume 1. (http://www.is.cityu.edu.hk/ejisdc.htm)

BMI-TechKnowledge, 2001, *Communication Technologies Handbook, 2001.* BMI-TechKnowledge Group (Pty) Ltd., Johannesburg, South Africa.

Brodnig, G. and Mayer-Schönberger, V., 2000, 'Bridging the Gap: The role of spatial information technologies in the integration of traditional environmental knowledge and western science.' *The Electronic Jour-*

nal on Information Systems in Developing Countries, Volume 1. (http://www.is.cityu.edu.hk/ejisdc.htm)

Burton, S., 2001, 'Msunduzi Community Network (Phase 1): An Evaluation Report.' IDRC, Johannesburg, South Africa (February, unpublished).

Byron, I. and Gagliardi, R., 1998, *Communities and the Information Society: The Role of Information and Communication Technologies in Education.* UNESCO, International Bureau of Education (IBE). (http://www.idrc.ca/acacia/studies/ir-unes.htm).

Camara, El Hadj H. and Thioune, R., 2001, 'Etude Pan africaine evaluation de projets d'introduction des TIC dans les écoles : cas des espaces cyber jeunes dans l'environnement scolaire sénégalais.' Acacia, IDRC, Dakar, Senegal (January, unpublished).

CEEWA, 2001, 'Consolidated Report on Monitoring Women Entrepreneurs in the ICT Project Sites (Nabweru, Buwama and Kampala).' Council for the Economic Empowerment of Women of Africa, Uganda (May, unpublished).

Cole, A., 1994, 'Information Technology and Gender. Problems and Proposals.' *Gender and Education,* 6(1), 77-84.

Credé, A. and Mansell, R., 1998, *Knowledge Societies ... in a Nutshell. Information Technologies for Sustainable Development,* IDRC, Ottawa, Canada.

Davison, R., Vogel, D., Harris, R., and Jones, N., 2000 *Technology Leapfrogging in Developing Countries: An Inevitable Luxury? The Electronic Journal on Information Systems in Developing Countries,* Volume 1. (http://www.is.cityu.edu.hk/ejisdc.htm).

Dieng, M., Sène, K., and Sow, Pape T., 2001, 'Etude Panafricaine sur les Télécentres/Sénégal,' Acacia, IDRC, Dakar, Senegal (May, unpublished).

Direction de l'aménagement du territoire du Sénégal, 1994, *Rapport d'avant-projet du schéma régional d'aménagement du territoire de Kaolack,* Commission Régionale d'Aménagement du Territoire de la Région de Kaolack, October.

Direction de l'aménagement du territoire du Sénégal, 1994, *Rapport d'avant-projet du schéma régional d'aménagement du territoire de Diourbel,* Commission Régionale d'Aménagement du Territoire de la Région de Diourbel, October.

Direction de l'aménagement du territoire du Sénégal, 1994, *Rapport d'avant-projet du schéma régional d'aménagement du territoire de Saint-Louis,*

Commission Régionale d'Aménagement du Territoire de la Région de Saint-Louis, October.

Direction de l'aménagement du territoire du Sénégal, 1994, *Rapport d'avant-projet du schéma régional d'aménagement du territoire de Tambacounda*, Commission Régionale d'Aménagement du Territoire de la Région de Tambacounda, October.

Etta, F., 2000, 'Technical Assessment of FASI Project Enhancing Women's Participation in Governance through Increased Access to Civic Information, Information and Communication Technologies,' IDRC, Nairobi, Kenya (April, unpublished).

Etta F., Aquinata A., and Salome K., 2001, 'A Study on Information and Communication Technologies and Community Development. Final Research Report,' IDRC, Nairobi, Kenya (unpublished).

Fluck, A.E., 1995 'Computers in Schools – a framework for development.' Discussion Paper from the Australian Computer Society and the Australian Council for Computers in Education. http://www.lare.tased.edu.au/acspaper/compsch1.htm

Hawkins, J., and Valentin, R., 1997, *Le développement à l'âge de l'information: Quatre scénarios pour l'avenir des technologies de l'information et des communications*. IDRC and Commission on Sciences and Technology for Development (UNO). http://www.idrc.ca/books/836/index.html

Institute of Economic Affairs, 2001, *Telecom Liberalisation: Empowering Kenyans in the Information Age*, IEA, Nairobi, Kenya.

International Telecommunications Unions, 1997, *Challenges to the Network: Telecoms and the Internet*, ITU, Geneva, Switzerland.

Katia, S., 2000, 'The Data Collection Exercise of the IDRC sponsored FASI Project Information Communication Technologies (ICTs) and Community Development Carried Out in Makueni District, Kenya.' IDRC, Nairobi, Kenya (December, unpublished).

Kemei, C. C., 2001, *Status of Telecoms in Kenya: A CCK Report*. Report for the Council for the Economic Empowerment of Women of Africa, Uganda.

Kibombo, R. and Kayambwe, S., 2000, 'A Baseline Study on Economic Empowerment of Women Through the Use of ICTs in Uganda.' Report for CEEWA, Uganda

Lohento, K., 2001, 'Maîtrise sociale des TIC en Afrique: Analyse d'expériences d'utilisation des NTIC.' www.beninnet.mailme.org; www.oridev.org

115

Makunja, C., 2000, 'Report of Document Analysis for the Study of Lessons Learned from ICTs and Community Development.' IDRC, Nairobi, Kenya (January, unpublished).

Mureithi, M., 2001, *Liberalising Telecommunications: A Policy and Regulatory Review*, June. Institute of Economic Affairs, Nairobi, Kenya.

Nath, V., 2000, *Heralding ICT Enabled Knowledge Societies: Way Forward for the Developing Countries*. Innovator, KnowNet Initiative, London School of Economics Inlaks Scholar (2000–2001), (http://www.vikasnath.org).

Ndiaye, A., 2000, 'Evaluation of "Décentralisation du Trade Point Sénégal" Project,' IDRC, Dakar, Senegal (November, unpublished).

Nor A., et al., 2000, 'Gender Differences in Computer Literacy Level Among Undergraduate Students in Universiti Kebangsaan Malaysia (UKM).' *The Electronic Journal on Information Systems in Developing Countries,* Volume 1. (http://www.is.cityu.edu.hk/ejisdc.htm).

OSIRIS, 2002, *L'Observatoire sur les Systèmes d'Information, les Réseaux et les Inforoutes au Sénégal,* Dakar, Senegal (http://www.osiris.sn).

Rathgeber, Eva M., 2000, 'Les femmes, les hommes et les technologies de l'information et des communications en Afrique: pourquoi il y a un problème d'inégalité des sexes.' In *L'inégalité des sexes et la révolution de l'information en Afrique*. Edited by Eva M. Rathgeber and Edith Ofwona Adera, IDRC, Ottawa, Canada. http://www.idrc.ca/acb/showprod.cfm?&DID=6&CATID=15&ObjectGroup_ID=40

Republic of Kenya, 2001, *Kakamega District Development Plan 1997-2001*, Office of the Vice-President and Ministry of Planning and National Development, Nairobi, Kenya.

Republic of Kenya, 1998, *Kenya Gazette Supplement No. 64 (Acts No 3),* ACTS, November 1998, Nairobi, Kenya.

Republic of Kenya, 2001, *Makueni District Development Plan 1997-2001*, Office of the Vice-President and Ministry of Planning and National Development, Nairobi, Kenya.

Sèye, R., Thioune, R. M., and Séne, K., 2000, 'Plan d'orientation méthodologique pour ELSA/ACACIA Etude TIC pour le Développement,' IDRC, Dakar, Senegal (September, unpublished).

Thioune, R. M., 2000 'Evaluation du projet d'introduction des TIC dans la gestion et la réhabilitation des terroirs villageois,' IDRC, Dakar, Senegal (November, unpublished).

Thioune, R. and Sène K., 2001, 'Technologies de l'information et de la communication et développement communautaire: leçons apprises de projets Acacia: Cas du Sénégal. Interim Report, Evaluation and Learning System for Acacia/ELSA,' IDRC, Dakar, Senegal (July, unpublished).

Uimonen, P., 1997, *Internet as a Tool for Social Development*. Department of Social Anthropology, Stockholm University, United Nations Research Institute for Social Development (UNRISD), Geneva. Paper Presented at the Annual Conference of the Internet Society, INET 97, Kuala Lumpur, 24–27 June 1997.

UNDP, 2001, *World Report on Human Development 2001*, United Nations Development Programme, De Boeck University for UNDP, Brussels, Belgium.

United States Department of Commerce, 1999, *National Trade Data Bank*, United States Department of Commerce, Washington, D.C. (3 September).

Whyte, A., 2000, *Assessing Community Telecentres: Guidelines for Research*, IDRC, Ottawa, Canada.

World Bank, 1999, *World Bank Development Report, 1999/2000: Entering the 21st Century*, The World Bank, Washington, D.C.

Ziliotto, A., 1989, *Qui sauvera le paysan africain?* Italian Association for International Development (AIDI), Catania, Italy.

The Publishers

The **International Development Research Centre** is a public corporation created by the Parliament of Canada in 1970 to help developing countries use science and technology to find practical, long-term solutions to the social, economic, and environmental problems they face. Support is directed toward developing an indigenous research capacity to sustain policies and technologies developing countries need to build healthier, more equitable, and more prosperous societies.

IDRC Books publishes research results and scholarly studies on global and regional issues related to sustainable and equitable development. As a specialist in development literature, IDRC Books contributes to the body of knowledge on these issues to further the cause of global understanding and equity. IDRC publications are sold through its head office in Ottawa, Canada, as well as by IDRC's agents and distributors around the world. The full catalogue is available at http://www.idrc.ca/booktique/.

CODESRIA is the Council for the Development of Social Science Research in Africa head-quartered in Dakar, Senegal. It is an independent organisation whose principal objectives are facilitating research, promoting research-based publishing and creating multiple forums geared towards the exchange of views and information among African researchers. It challenges the fragmentation of research through the creation of thematic research networks that cut across linguistic and regional boundaries.

CODESRIA publishes a quarterly journal, *Africa Development*, the longest standing Africa-based social science journal; *Afrika Zamani*, a journal of history; the *African Sociological Review*, *African Journal of International Affairs (AJIA)* and *Identity, Culture and Politics: An Afro-Asian Dialogue*. Research results and other activities of the institution are disseminated through 'Working Papers', 'Monograph Series', 'New Path Series', 'State-of-the-Literature Series', 'CODESRIA Book Series', and the *CODESRIA Bulletin*.